A GUIDE TO PUBLIC ETHICS

A GUIDE TO
Public Ethics

William Fox

JUTA

A Guide to Public Ethics
First published 2010

Juta and Company Ltd
First floor
Sunclare Building
21 Dreyer Street
Claremont
7708

ISBN: 978-0-70217-762-0

Project Manager: Marlinee Chetty
Editor: Alfred LeMaitre
Proofreader: Rae Dalton
Typesetter: Guinea*folio*
Indexer: Daphne Burger
Cover designer: Marius Roux
Printed in South Africa by Mills Litho

Cartoon Credits: Special thanks to Alistair Findlay – p 21; Brandan Reynolds, Editorial Cartoonist, Business Day – p 96; Dr Jack – pp 17, 169; Cuan Miles – pp 1, 41, 68, 134; Sifiso Yalo – p 53; Zapiro – p 121.

This book has been peer reviewed by critical readers.

Set in Minion Pro 11.3 pt on 14pt

DEDICATION

To Doreen for having enough patience to let me come to the end of the book.

To my children for cheering me on.

To my grandchildren for their faith in me, although I don't deserve it.

To my great-grandchild; may he grow up to be an academic.

To my publisher, Mthunzi Nxawe, for believing that this book is necessary.

CONTENTS

FOREWORD

This book was written in the knowledge that the issue of ethics is being debated in many forums all over South Africa. It is a phenomenon that a multitude of ethical questions are retarding many aspects of transformation on the way to nation-building in the country. There are many perceptions about ethics in general and about public ethics in particular. As the South African Constitution requires that government should be transparent, many cases of unethical behaviour are being highlighted on a daily basis. This does not mean that unethical behaviour is more prevalent in the public sector, but merely that the public sector has to perform transparently, which is important because all citizens have a vested interest in the way government and government agencies act or fail to act.

The main objective of the book is not to give a comprehensive view of the entire phenomenon of public ethics, but merely to highlight a good number of the most important aspects and to create an impression of the vast field to be covered and the ethical minefield in which selected and appointed public officials have to move on a daily basis.

The foundation of public ethics is the South African Constitution. This document is a guide to the way in which democratic governments in all spheres, and their agencies, should conduct their day-to-day business, which is to deliver public goods and service to the whole of South African society in an effective and efficient and a responsive, developmental and sustainable way. The legacy of racial discrimination in South Africa, which lasted for at least three centuries, cannot be erased in a matter of fifteen years, but that does not mean that the basic norms, values and principles provided in the Constitution should be ignored or misinterpreted.

Each chapter of the book starts with a column headed 'In This Chapter'. This is not a full index of what is included in that chapter, but merely gives an indication of the main objectives to be covered. Also, each chapter ends with the column headed 'The Principles, Values and Norms Presented in this Chapter'. Again, this is not a comprehensive listing of all of the principles, values and norms contained in that chapter, but merely an indication of what the reader may expect to find in the chapter and make a quick evaluation of what is important to her or him.

Some of the discussions may seem long-winded and irrelevant, but it was necessary to describe the sources of basic ethical considerations and their development over time. Likewise, the sources of democratic thought, and its development over time, have been explained in order to understand how South Africa came to its present political dispensation. In many cases, the discussion draws on selected online resources; full details are provided in the text (including the URL of each website), and in the References section, to allow interested readers to explore these topics in greater depth than is possible here.

The South African Constitution is largely based on the principles and values of Western cultures and democratic experience over many centuries. However, post-colonial and true African thought are also present, as is evident from the applied *Batho Pele* principles and the culture of *Ubuntu*.

In an attempt to give a more practical view of public ethics, the chapters contain many cases and the findings of a number of research projects and investigations. These give an idea of the present state of South African public ethics and the way in which it could or should develop.

Hopefully, the book will stimulate readers to make a wider examination of the many sources available on the subject of public ethics. The book itself should give students and practitioners in public management a solid grounding on which to build further and deeper knowledge in this field. This is not only important for the present, but is imperative for the future to which the South African nation aspires.

William Fox
Hermanus
May 2010

Chapter 1

Introduction

IN THIS CHAPTER

After reading this chapter, you should be able to:

- define ethics;
- explain the concepts of principles, values and norms;
- define public ethics;
- discuss the meaning of democracy;
- understand the South African context of public ethics;
- gain a perspective on South African morality.

Before studying this chapter, see if you can answer the following question:
How would you define the terms *ethics*, *principles*, *norms* and *values*, or do they have the same meaning?

Like taxis, the gravy train always has room for more.

1.1 Orientation

Human beings attain habits right from their birth. Most human actions are based on habits. Most humans are able to change their actions at will, especially when they find that they are detrimental to their natural and social environments. The term 'ethos' means a shared or a personal habit, which refers to a way of choosing what is right and what is wrong or merely as a way of life. Habits may be taught, attained or be intuitive, but they can be studied as well.

An interesting phenomenon of present-day public service is the vast interest that is paid to matters of ethics all over the world, especially in the USA, but also in emerging democratic cultures like that of South Africa. This interest is not confined to academics but also includes the media, public officials and non-governmental organisations. South Africa has one of the most liberal constitutions on earth, and yet reports on unethical behaviour surface on a regular basis. This is being revealed because the South African Constitution guarantees freedom of speech.

The media in the country and non-governmental institutions and community-based institutions are continuously monitoring the state of ethics in the country. As the Executive Head of the Ethics Institute of South Africa, Willem Landman (*Die Burger*, 21 May 2009) emphasises that the public's right to information forms the basis of a sound democracy. Secrecy and ignorance create gaps within which a government is able to treat its citizens inconsistently or even to ignore their interests. It could be added that misinformation spread by a government usually covers up unethical behaviour.

Landman holds that public figures, in a certain sense, forego their right to privacy. Responsibility and authority have been entrusted to them in order for them to act in everybody's best interests. Citizens have a right to know whether political leaders live up to the standards, values, responsibilities and character they expect from politicians. Landman adds that politicians are not expected to be moral icons. Rather, it is a matter of citizens knowing whether their elected and appointed leaders, in their public and private lives, are not liars, swindlers or abusers of women, or whether they have reckless habits. They can then judge whether those leaders are worthy of the trust placed in them. Public figures choose to be in the limelight and are at risk that their private lives could be made public. If they wish to avoid this, they have to ensure that their private lives are beyond reproach.

If we could hypothesise, we could state that democracy enhances public ethics. With this in mind, and regarding South Africa's position, we could ask whether democracy is possible in emerging societies. Also, in South Africa's case, we could contrast the terms of South Africa's Constitution with the ethical status of its public service, or formulate this as a question: what is the relationship between public ethics and democracy in present-day South Africa? In order to answer these questions, this book aims to define the most basic terms in the context of ethics and democracy and how they interplay in our time. Therefore, the origins of ethics and democracy and their interplay need to be described briefly. In the latter case, I will briefly explore South Africa's transition from a largely totalitarian system of government to what may be termed a democratic dispensation. Lastly, we will seek to find a way forward in which public ethics could be enhanced.

Over the past number of years, the South African government has enacted legislation and created institutions in an attempt to curb corrupt and dishonest acts and behaviour. These measures include the following: Prevention and Combating of Corrupt Activities (Act 12 of 2004); Promotion of Access to Information (Act 2 of 2000); Promotion of Administrative Justice (Act 3 of 2000); Protective Disclosures (Act 26 of 2000); Public Finance Management (Act 1 of 1999); Municipal Finance Management (Act 56 of 2003); and Financial Intelligence Centre (Act 38 of 2001); as well as initiatives such as the Public Service Anti-Corruption Strategy and in the case of the Public Protector in practice and codes of conduct for the public service, provincial governments and local governments. In spite of all this, it is generally believed by the public at large that unethical behaviour in the public sector has reached endemic proportions.

1.2 Defining public ethics

Ethics, as a branch of philosophy, is considered a normative science, because it is concerned with norms of human conduct, as distinguished from the formal sciences, such as mathematics and logic, and the empirical sciences, such as chemistry and physics. However, the empirical social sciences, including psychology, to a certain extent impinge on the concerns of ethics to the extent that they study social behaviour. For example, in certain cases the social sciences attempt to determine the relation of particular ethical principles to social behaviour and to investigate the cultural conditions that contribute to the formation of such principles.

The term 'ethics' is derived from the ancient Greek word *ethika*, which in a general sense means the study of habits. Studies of how humans choose to act focus on our behaviour and ask others, and ourselves, who should be held responsible for it. However the two most essential questions in ethics are, firstly, how can we distinguish between good and evil?; and secondly, why should we be good? We often intend to do what we do, and therefore ethics examines how we develop those intentions with a view to attaining our objectives. Humans often intend doing 'the right thing', but instead do something misguided or unintended. However, in those cases we revisit the facts, analyse them and endeavour to learn from our mistakes.

Ethics may be defined as the philosophical study of the nature of good, virtue, right and other morally relevant terms. In this sense, morally relevant merely refers to accepted standards of right and wrong. In Western culture, reflection on the nature of morality began in ancient Greece in the 5th century BC. The Greeks were aware of the different moral customs of other peoples, as well as the differences that existed within the various Greek city-states. The awareness of diversity among customs led them to consider whether any moral practices could be regarded as better than others.

Ethics may also be defined as a system of moral principles and the rules of conduct recognised in respect of a particular class of human actions or governing, say, a particular society, community, organisation, culture or group – for example, medical ethics. It is also the branch of philosophy dealing with values in respect of human conduct, regarding the values relating to human conduct in terms of the rightness or wrongness of actions and the goodness and badness of motives and ends. It could also refer to the moral principles of an individual.

In short, then, ethics may be regarded as a system of moral principles and rules of conduct. Terms such as **principles**, **norms** and **values** are often used in conjunction or synonymous with the concept of ethics. However, as Covey (1992:35) points out, principles are not values. The character ethic, according to Covey (1992:32) is based on the fundamental idea that there are principles that direct human effectiveness. These are natural laws that are just as real, unchanging and unarguable in the human dimension as natural laws such as gravity. Principles in the public domain are not, or should not be, religious, esoteric or mysterious ideas. Such principles are self-evident. Covey (1992:34) refers to examples such as fairness, integrity, honesty, human dignity, service, quality, excellence, potential and growth.

Public ethics refers to the area of ethics regarding the matter of how humans choose to live together within the many networks of relationships that comprise the sum of our lives. A number of ethical questions may be termed 'private', to which the individual has to pay attention and which cannot or can hardly be taken over by anyone else – for example, exercise and nutrition. Other ethical questions are common to both the public and private domains, such as when we act with our family or partner, or as a friend. In a more public sense would be our driving, the actions we approve or disapprove and our neighbourhood actions. Some spheres of public ethics have led to the formulation of standards of practice – for example, most types of work are evaluated as well or poorly done (not up to standard), in light of the current standards of practice. When we do not know what those standards are, we may inquire and receive answers. When the current standards of practice are strictly upheld by some, partially upheld by some and ignored by others, we could choose to relate to any one of the groups. Some standards of practice are developed as rules, regulations and laws that bind everybody – for example, building codes, traffic laws and professional rules of conduct.

There are cases where laws have been made requiring certain standards of practice or prohibiting certain kinds of practices regarded as harmful to the public or harmful to the trust on which government depends. Even in such cases where no law has been made or where no law could ever be made, the public ethics of the people who live in communities, day by day, act by setting expectations, laying down boundaries and expressing praise and gratitude for those who uphold the public interest and act faithfully for the sake of the community. They also express blame and disapproval towards those whose words or deeds show disrespect for justice in the community and the best interests of citizens.

In its fullest sense, the public ethics of a community provide the moral habits within which everyone lives, holding themselves and others accountable when it is proper to do so, rejecting corrupted, narrow actions and favouritism, but also praising acceptable actions. In this sense, public ethics is basic to what is written into law and what cannot be written into law. It constitutes the moral quality of what is shared, lived and felt by the people living within a specific environment. When this quality is weak, fragmented and confusing, it will seem to support many kinds of actions, or no actions will be ruled out or in. Therefore, no one standard will actually apply to anything. In its worst sense, a slapdash attitude will prevail. However, when the public ethic is fairly strong, and is voiced at timely intervals and demonstrated by noticeable and praised actions, it supports those who strive to live morally correct lives, and denies support to those who choose to act detrimentally towards others.

Although private ethics does not form part of this book, it is pertinent when, for example, companies gain uncompetitive access to goods and services in a way that is not clearly illegal. Also, cases of public ethics focus not only on public officials but also on those who see public officials as lobbying targets, such as when particular political parties or individuals are favoured at elections. One more example that does not focus on public officials is the matter of citizenship. In spite of the devotion of officials towards the best interests of citizens, no elected or appointed public official is able to do much if citizens themselves do not care, are apathetic, cannot be reached or expect someone else to ensure the quality of their lives. No democracy is able to survive without some degree of civic activity by citizens. The broad area of public ethics cannot be safeguarded by any one institution (and South Africa has many organisations and research projects at various universities investigating the phenomenon), but depends on the country's citizenship as a whole.

Principles are fundamental guidelines for human conduct that have been proven to have enduring and permanent value. The way to explain the self-evident nature of principles is to consider the preposterous proposal of attempting to live an effective life based on the opposites, such as unfairness, deceit, baseness, uselessness and mediocrity. There seems to be an acceptance that there is some quick and easy way to achieve quality of life without going through the natural process of work and growth which makes it possible. This is the scheme that promises achievement without work. It may appear to succeed, but it is the schemer that remains. Such a work ethic is illusory and deceptive, and trying to achieve high-quality results with 'quick fixes' is about as effective as trying to get somewhere in a city using another city's map.

It is a generally accepted fact that no particular conception of **democracy** is the only correct one, i.e. the one to which all people have to adhere if they are not considered immoral or irrational. The validity of democracy depends on the degree to which it is generally understood and accepted. Many people, from strict socialists to stern liberalists, do not use the term 'democracy' in exactly the same sense. However, for the purposes of this book – and aimed particularly at South Africa – defining the term is necessary in order to pursue the investigation into public ethics. Therefore the basic definition formulated by Ranney (1975:307) is appropriate for our purposes:

Democracy is a form of government organised in accordance with the principles of popular sovereignty, political equality, popular consultation, and majority rule.

The principle of popular sovereignty requires that basic governmental policy- and decision-making authority be vested in all members of the community and not in any particular person or ruling class. This principle forms the nucleus of the conception of democracy, while the other three are logical elaborations. One general feature of modern nations is their command of full and exclusive legal power to make and enforce laws for the people within the territories under their jurisdiction. This sovereign power is located somewhere in a country's political governmental structure, but the importance of this is that in a democracy it has to be vested in all members of society.

As far as the term 'vested in the people' is concerned, the principle of popular sovereignty does not require that all the people directly make all the daily decisions of government. The people in a democracy, like the dictator in a dictatorship, may delegate part of their decision-making power to legislators, executives, judges or to anybody they wish. The people remain sovereign as long as they themselves have the power to decide such matters as what decision-making powers are to be delegated to whom, under what conditions of accountability and for what period of time. When ultimate power is vested in one person, the government is a dictatorship or an autocracy. When it is vested in some members of the community, they constitute a ruling class and the government is what is termed an oligarchy or aristocracy. The government is a democracy only when ultimate power is vested in all the people.

The term '**the people**' needs to be clarified. In a democracy, power rests in all *members of society*. The term 'society' in this sense means something more than an aggregation of people, but implies a kind of bond, shared values, as well as some mutual interests, feelings and behaviour. The term 'member' implies a certain kind of relationship between an individual and a group, involving both certain privileges from the group and certain obligations to it. For example, a person's right to vote and hold office is determined by the community's judgment of the ability and willingness of that person to fulfil the obligation of loyalty to the community and of obedience to its laws. In such a nation, children are usually excluded from voting because they are deemed incapable of fulfilling obligations like loyalty and obedience. Aliens and convicted criminals are usually excluded because they are deemed unwilling to accept these obligations. Of course, not all communities agree on these issues. Some argue that it is undemocratic to exclude children, and in South Africa's case prisoners have been allowed to vote. However, in democratic nations the willingness to accept certain obligations is regarded as the proper standard for determining who should and who should not be part of the sovereign people.

The principle of **political equality** requires that each member of society has the same opportunities as every other to participate in the nation's political decision-making processes. In simple terms the principle means 'one person, one vote', but it also guarantees many other matters: eligible voters must be allowed to vote and their votes counted and given equal weight; genuine alternatives must be put before voters so that they may make real choices; all members of the community must have an equal opportunity to ascertain what those alternatives are, and the arguments for and against each alternative; and they must have an equal opportunity to persuade others (and be persuaded) of the desirability of each alternative. The principle of political equality means equal *opportunities* for all the members of society, not actual participation.

The principle of **popular consultation** comprises two requirements. Firstly, a democratic action must have some kind of institutional machinery through which public officials learn what public policies the people wish to be adopted and enforced. Secondly, having ascertained what public policies are preferred by the people, public officials must then put them into effect whether they believe them to be wise or not. So, when public officials know and implement what the people (and not they) want, the people (and not they) are sovereign. This means that the claim of a particular policy to the title 'democratic' is determined by how it is made, rather than by its content. Content enters the picture only when it directly affects the nature of the decision-making processes.

The principle of **majority rule** has proven to be the most controversial of all. In a democracy, this principle requires that should a decision by government be made against the ultimate desires of the popular majority, but should there be a general disagreement, the government should act on the desires of even a slight majority rather than on those of the smaller number. Some political commentators argue that as long as the procedures employed to make governmental decisions are constantly approved by at least 50 per cent plus one of the people, and as long as that same proportion of the people may at any time revise those procedures, the principle of majority rule is satisfied (see Ranney, 1975:310).

A number of commentators contend that unlimited majority rule is incompatible with true democracy: for example, when the majority transfers sovereignty from the people to a dictator, prohibiting certain people from expressing their political views or abolishing elections. Therefore, these commentators argue that unlimited majority rule cannot be considered a principle of true majority rule. However, Ranney (1975:312) argues that the only restraints on popular majorities are those imposed by majorities on themselves and removable at any time without restraint by majorities.

The basis of public ethics in South Africa is the Constitution of the Republic of South Africa, 1996. The preamble to the Constitution, on behalf of the people of South Africa, recognises the injustices of the past and believes that South Africa belongs to everyone who lives in it. The Constitution was adopted as the supreme law of the country in order to heal the divisions that were built up over many years and to establish a society based on **democratic** values, to lay the foundations for an open society in which government is based on the will of the people and every citizen is equally protected by law, and to build a united and democratic country.

The Greek philosopher, Aristotle, established democracy as a political concept, as opposed to the aristocracy prevalent in his time. In modern times, his concept of democracy may be contrasted with autocracy, which is based on authoritarianism. The present concept of Aristotle's formulation of democracy is what is understood as participatory democracy (see Gildenhuys, 1993:51), in which every citizen enjoys the right to participate directly in the process of political decision-making, and so also enjoys direct participation in the process of policy-making. Shades of this type of democracy are found in South Africa in the propagation of maximum political participation in local government affairs and the devolution of power to autonomous self-governing local authorities.

The problem with participatory democracy is that it is suitable only for very small local communities, but cannot effectively be applied to larger local communities and even less to national states. However, the philosophy behind participatory democracy established the principle of the right of the individual voter to participate directly in the public decision-making process.

It is clear that modern public ethics are based on a democratic way of thinking so that countries may once again take their rightful place among the family of nations. As explained in this book, the concept of democracy is not easy to define. This concept originated in Athens in the 5th century BC. At that time, its central doctrine was that every free-born male citizen should participate directly in making laws and public decisions, and that this function should not be delegated to others. In modern times, the term has developed widely different, even opposing, meanings.

1.3 Norms and values

In the context of this book, norms are the standards or patterns that are typical of a given community, and the members of that community are expected to adapt to its norms. The values of a community are usually defined as the moral or professional standards or principles of behaviour expected of the members of that community.

1.4 South African context

The first proof of the existence of our forbears, the australopithecines, and of their journey from the tropical forests of Africa to South Africa millions of years ago, was discovered in South Africa by Dart and Broom (see Giliomee & Mbenga, 2007). Although this discovery was first viewed with scepticism, just like Leakey's discovery of the origins of modern humans in East Africa in the 1930s, it is now a generally accepted fact. The later early inhabitants of South Africa were the San and the Khoi-Khoi. The San originally were hunter-gatherers, while the Khoi-Khoi originally were pastoralists. Their pastoral economy brought relative riches to individuals and communities, but it was also unstable and they constantly had to find new pastures.

It seems that the Khoi-Khoi community was fairly individualistic. There were clear channels for upward and downward mobility. Theoretically, political power was based on heredity succession, but the power of rulers was determined by how well they themselves were able to accumulate livestock and protect those of their followers.

During the first centuries of the second millennium the ancestors of the Nguni and Sotho-Tswana speakers entered South Africa (Giliomee & Mbenga, 2007:28–29). They probably moved from the African Lakes region because of a dryer climate that occurred between 900 and 1200. Nguni farmers moved to the grasslands in the interior during the 1300s. Other groups slowly moved into the interior. For example, the Kwena probably moved south of the Vaal River in about the mid-1600s.

The origins of black political communities during the early Iron Age show two conflicting processes: **segmentation** and **differentiation**. When a group divides into two or more divisions it is called segmentation. This could be due to sons marrying and starting on their own or when natural resources became limited, although they remained related to each other. Segmentation is a natural, continuing process. Differentiation is the process by which certain individuals or groups assume political, social and economic power over others. In pre-colonial societies this resulted in three social categories: chiefs, common members of the community and clients.

In almost all South African communities, the place of residence constituted the basic social and economic unit. Except in extraordinary circumstances, the eldest man was the head of the household. He had a great deal of power in the fields of religion, economy and social relationships, among others. His authority was derived from his genealogical seniority, and the status of the other men in the household also rested on their genealogical status. Women, like children, also had rights and obligations but were regarded as perpetual minors and had no voice in the matters of the household. They could not inherit or transfer material goods of any importance. Chiefs exercised the same duties as the head of the household, but covered a wider area (Giliomee & Mbenga, 2007:34).

The economic control powers of the head of the household were based on the wealth that he had inherited from his ancestors. He had control of the allocation of agricultural land and of livestock. Because he owned the *lobola* (dowry) cattle, he controlled social relationships such as weddings.

Various related households formed a line of descent. When necessary, they gave each other support and advice. After several generations we could possibly recognise such ties only through similar names, laudations or (especially among the Sotho-Tswana) totems. Such mutual customs present clan bonds. Clans did not enjoy the same tight bonds. Some bonds were extremely tight – for example, because an individual or a family was regarded as a chief or as superior. Other clans were loosely bound because newcomers, aliens or fugitives were accepted. Therefore, some clans were controlled by a strong or accepted chief, while in others the chief mainly had a ritual or religious role. Therefore, when a chief allocated agricultural land, ordered the first harvest, waged war or brought offerings after a victory, he acted on behalf of a community of heads of households. However, there was no direct connection between clans and the occupancy of an area.

The position of the chief as the exclusive owner of the land, the people and property held the seeds of hierarchy and dominance. Chiefs were richer than the common people and used their positions of power to become richer. They were able to claim tributaries and labour from their followers. They could also lay charges of witchcraft and invoke hereditary laws to appropriate the riches of their people. However, chiefs were not rejected as authoritarian or tyrannical. They were expected to apply laws, protect the community in times of danger, supply food in time of famine and call upon the forefathers. Politically, they had to be astute or even cunning but, by and large, they knew that there were limits to their actions, and fraternal competition also brought pressure to bear (Giliomee & Mbenga, 2007:35).

Before the creation of permanent chiefships, circa 1800, all chiefs relied on the support of their communities. Therefore they had to keep their communities contented. A knowledgeable chief seldom challenged the will of his people. He mainly consulted his people and elders. Many brutal or greedy chiefs were simply bypassed, or rejected and superseded (Giliomee & Mbenga, 2007:35).

In South African communities, from ancient times, people lived by a system of values called *Ubuntu*. As shall be seen later, *Ubuntu* is a comprehensive value system aimed at the ideal of everyone being a good person. It has been, and still is, typical of African and specifically South African culture. Its core principle is that everyone should care for one another's wellbeing and live in a spirit of mutual support. Therefore, *Ubuntu* is an all-inclusive, deep-rooted African world-view, which pursues the primary values of intense humanness, caring, sharing and compassion and associated values, ensuring a happy and qualitative human community life in a family atmosphere and spirit.

1.5 Perspective on South African public ethics

In considering the current South African scene, as far as the general ethical conduct of its citizens is concerned, one gets a gloomy picture. In a statement on fraud and corruption, former President Thabo Mbeki stated: '... it would seem to me that many of our society are inspired by a system of values which begins and ends with a pursuit of what is materially beneficial to themselves, with no sense of what is morally correct'. He added: 'No questions are asked about the ethical behaviour of any of us, as part of determining whether we should indeed be emulated or not. Success is defined as success in having addressed effectively the material needs of the human being … What I am trying to suggest is that our society evolved in a manner which gave birth to a situation in which a disastrous collapse of social values occurred, to be replaced by the notion that what is good is what serves my individual material interests and pleasures.' (www.saiga.co.za)

Jeffreys states that where there are people, corruption will surface at one time or another (*Die Burger*, 21 May 2009). The question is, what is being done about it? As an example, he relates the case of the Speaker of the British House of Commons, who resigned his office because he did not act strongly enough against Members of Parliament who abused the allowance system. There is no indication that the Speaker himself was guilty, but being responsible, overall, for these abuses, he resigned – the first time in 300 years that this has happened. Action was being taken against the guilty parties, and what Jeffreys does not mention is that some of them had also resigned. This is a good example of democratic responsibility. Jeffreys draws a distinction between this example and the present situation in South Africa. Corruption is endemic in South Africa and may never be conquered, but it should be fought with all the means at the citizens' disposal. Above all, democratic transparency is necessary. However, he concludes that there seems to be a lack of political will in South Africa.

An attempt has been made to test people's morality; this was the so-called moral intelligence test. Since the days of the old tests of intelligence, many new theories on intelligence have been developed (Naudé, 2008). The narrow cognitive focus of traditional IQ tests has been extended to include performance and ability – for example, emotional, kinetic, artistic, mental and cultural intelligence. From this, Naudé investigates the possibility of a so-called moral intelligence.

Criticism against linking intelligence to morality is that its measurement is problematic and therefore cannot be applied to people on a comparative basis. How, for example, do we measure whether one person is 'more moral' than the other? The heavy burden carried by *intelligence*, in the sense of 'cognitive ability' does not explain the fact that clever people could also be corrupt – for example, in what is termed white-collar crime. Also, there is the problem that touches on all intelligence: to what extent should cultural influence be taken into account? Although there are actually ways to measure people's ethical reasoning abilities, this is restricted to a theoretical level and does not imply that individuals with a high performance mark will actually behave as such. There is no guarantee that a student who obtains 80 per cent in a professional ethics test will actually behave ethically.

Ethical behaviour has also been influenced by globalisation. Globalisation in its cultural form implies that we are living on an ever-shrinking globe. Since 1948, we have actually been discussing universal human rights that may be applied across cultural boundaries. Therefore, there are grounds on which to base 'moral intelligence'. This refers to the moral dimensions of the situation and the ability to resolve dilemmas by ethically acceptable means. There are at least three factors that are, jointly, present in morally intelligent people (Naudé, 2008). These are discussed in the following section.

1.5.1 Moral education

A healthy moral education is present when the positive conventions of the community become a part of our everyday activities. First we have the pre-conventional phase, in which children do not yet understand what is expected of them and act 'ethically' in fear of punishment. This is followed by the conventional phase, in which people start internalising and replicating positive expectations because they understand the interests of others around them. A small number also reach the post-conventional phase, in which the interests of all people are respected and normal ethical expectations are exceeded. In a healthy moral education, with the assistance of parents, the school, friends, religion and the community, moral intelligence increases. Good manners are instilled and eventually become part of one's character. It makes us capable 'to know' what to do in a situation requiring ethical decision-making without necessarily having to resort to a long process of reasoning. The reverse is also true: without adequate moral education, people are trapped in pre-conventional behaviour. In their actions they display low moral intelligence and an inability to perceive the moral quality of situations and make sound decisions. What makes it difficult is that they only act 'ethically' when they believe the chances of being caught out and punished exceed the risk of their planned (bad) actions.

1.5.2 Moral intelligence

Moral intelligence is the capacity to understand right from wrong, which means that people should have strong ethical convictions and to act on them so that they behave in the right and honourable way. It promotes the so-called 'seven essential virtues' of empathy, conscience, self-control, respect, kindness, tolerance and fairness from both a Christian and a global (post-modern) perspective.

PRINCIPLES, VALUES AND NORMS PRESENTED IN THIS CHAPTER

Popular sovereignty
People
Vestment in the people
Popular consultation
Majority rule
Public accountability
Moral and intelligence education
Empathy
Conscience
Self-control
Tolerance
Fairness
Respect
Altruism

Having studied this chapter, how would you now answer the question posed at the beginning?
Give your answer in the form of a critical essay of about 500 words, and explain the similarities and differences in the terms *ethics, principles, norms* and *values.*

Chapter 2

Foundations of modern-day ethics

IN THIS CHAPTER

After reading this chapter, you should be able to:

- consider the nature of ethical principles;
- give a brief history of ethical thinking
- discuss early Greek and Roman ethics
- highlight aspects of religious ethics;
- summarise the main trends in secular ethical philosophies;
- point to contemporary trends.

Before studying this chapter, see if you can answer the following question:
What is the range of sources on which modern-day ethics is based?

Some are more equal before the law than others.

2.1 Introduction

Ethics (*ethika* in Greek, from ethos, meaning 'character', 'custom') are principles or standards of human conduct. Ethics are sometimes called morals (*mores* in Latin, meaning 'customs'). By extension, this refers to the study of such principles, which is also called moral philosophy. This book is concerned with ethics in both senses of the term, but chiefly in the latter sense. The discussion is not only confined to that of Western civilization but also to the South African context in its widest perspective, as every culture has developed an ethic of is own. However, as far as South Africa is concerned, the South African Constitution forms the foundation of public ethics, and the principles and values it contains are obviously based on the Western style of democracy.

In the context of this book, ethics is defined as the philosophical study of the nature of good, right and other morally relevant terms. In this regard, terms such as principles, morals and values are also used, often in a synonymous sense. However, as pointed out, principles are self-evident guidelines for human conduct that have been proven to have enduring and permanent value. It is usually accepted that, in Western culture, contemplation of the nature of morality began in ancient Greece with the Sophists, during the 5th century BC. The Sophists were teachers who claimed that they could teach anyone to demonstrate the moral acceptability of any given cause. The Sophists had their opponents, of whom Socrates was the most prominent.

Philosophers have attempted to determine goodness in conduct according to two chief principles and have considered certain types of conduct either good in themselves or good because they conform to a particular moral standard. The former implies a final value, or *summum bonum*, which is a Latin expression (meaning 'highest good') used to describe the most important end that people ought to pursue (refer to en.wikipedia.org/wiki/Summum_bonum). The *summum bonum* is thought of as both being an end in itself and as containing all other goods.

Desires are mostly conflicting and all of them cannot be pursued; therefore some goods have to be foregone in order to acquire others. Hence it is necessary to evaluate the relative value of desired goods and of finally deciding which of them have to be obtained at the loss of the others. Goods can be divided into two categories: happiness and virtue – the physical and the moral. It is relatively easy to determine, within each category, what the relation of certain good things to one another is, but it is difficult to determine the relative superiority of the categories of virtue and happiness. If virtue and happiness are mutually exclusive, a crucial choice has to be made between them.

2.2 Ethical principles

Depending on the social setting, the authority evoked for good conduct was seen as the will of a deity, the pattern of nature or the rule of reason. When the will of a deity was the authority, obedience to the divine commandments in scriptural texts was the accepted standard of conduct. If the pattern of nature was the authority, conformity to the qualities attributed to human nature was the standard. When reason ruled, behaviour was expected to result from rational thought.

Sometimes, principles are chosen of which the ultimate value is not determined, because it is believed that such a determination is impossible. Such an ethical philosophy usually equates satisfaction in life with prudence, pleasure or power. However, it is basically derived from belief in the ethical doctrine of natural human fulfilment as an ultimate good. Someone lacking motivation to exercise preference may be resigned to accepting all customs, and therefore may develop a philosophy of prudence. That person then lives in conformity with the moral conduct of the period and society.

Hedonism is that philosophy in which the highest good is *pleasure*. Hedonists decide between the most enduring pleasures or the most intense pleasures, whether present pleasures should be denied for the sake of overall comfort, and whether mental pleasures are preferable to physical pleasures.

A philosophy in which the highest attainment is *power* may result in competition. As each victory tends to raise the level of competition, the logical end of such a philosophy is unlimited or results in absolute power. Power-seekers may not accept customary ethical rules but may conform to other rules that could help them to become successful. They will seek to persuade others that they are moral in the accepted sense of the term in order to mask their power motives and to gain the ordinary rewards of morality.

2.3 A brief history

For as long as people have been living together in groups, the moral regulation of behaviour has been necessary for the group's wellbeing. Although morals were formalised and made into arbitrary standards of conduct, they developed, sometimes irrationally, after religious taboos were violated, or out of chance behaviour that became habit and then custom, or from laws imposed by chiefs to prevent disharmony in their tribes. Even the ancient Egyptian and Sumerian civilisations did not develop any systemised ethics: maxims and precepts laid down by secular leaders mingled with a strict religion that affected the behaviour of every Egyptian. In ancient China the maxims of Confucius were accepted as a moral code. The Greek philosophers, beginning in about the 6th century BC, theorised intensively about moral behaviour, which led to the further development of philosophical ethics.

2.3.1 Early Greek ethics

In the Hellenistic world, philosophy was divided into three parts: logic, physics and ethics (see Boardman *et al*, 2001:365–368). The task of ethics is to analyse human wellbeing and to establish the conditions under which that may be achieved. In general, the various schools of philosophy were in agreement: as indicated, reflection on the nature of morality began in Greece with the Sophists in the 5th century BC. According to the philosopher Epicurus, we should base choice and avoidance on the health of our bodies and tranquillity of our souls, as that is the objective of a happy life. A group known as the Stoics acknowledged the same ideal by seeking to expel all passions that disturb the mind: desire, delight, fear and grief.

In the 6th century BC, the Greek philosopher Pythagoras developed one of the earliest moral philosophies, from Orphism, a Greek mystic religion. Believing that the intellectual nature is superior to the sensual nature and that the best life is one devoted to mental discipline, he founded a semi-religious order with rules emphasising simplicity in speech, dress and food. Members observed rituals that were designed to demonstrate the decreed ethical beliefs.

In the 5th century BC, the Sophists, who taught rhetoric, logic and civil affairs, were sceptical of moral absolutes. Protagoras taught that human judgment is subjective, and that one's perception is valid only to oneself. Gorgias went to the extreme of arguing that nothing exists; that if anything does exist, human beings could not know it; and that if they did know it, they could not communicate that knowledge. Other Sophists believed that might made right.

Socrates opposed the Sophists. His philosophical position may be

The tail trying to wag the donkey.

summarised as follows: virtue is knowledge; people will be virtuous if they know what virtue is; and vice, or evil, is the result of ignorance. Therefore, according to Socrates, education could make people moral.

2.3.2 Greek schools of ethics

Four schools of moral philosophy originated among the disciples of Socrates:

- The Cynics maintained that the essence of virtue (the only good) is self-control, and that it is capable of being taught. They disdained pleasure as an evil, if accepted as a guideline to conduct. They considered all pride as a vice, including pride in appearance of cleanliness.
- The Cyrenaics were hedonists, postulating pleasure as the chief good (provided that it does not dominate our lives); that no kind of pleasure is superior to another; and that it is measurable only in degree and duration.
- The Megarians held that although good may be called God or reason, it is 'one', and that good is the final secret of the universe, which can be revealed only through logical inquiry.
- The Platonists shared Plato's view that good was an essential element of reality. Evil does not exist in itself but is, to be more precise, an imperfect reflection, which is good.

During the first half of the 4th century BC, Plato argued that human virtue lay in the fitness of a person to perform that person's proper function on earth. The human soul has three elements: intellect, will and emotion, each of which possesses a specific virtue in the good person and performs a specific role. The virtue of intellect is wisdom, or knowledge of the ends of life. The virtue of the emotions is temperance or self-control. Justice, the ultimate virtue, is the harmonious relation of all the others, each part of the soul doing its appropriate task and keeping its proper place. Plato held that the intellect should be sovereign, the will second and the emotions subject to intellect and will. Therefore, the just person, whose life is ordered in this way, is the good person.

During the late 4th century BC, Aristotle, in the *Nicomachean Ethics*, regarded happiness as the aim of life. He defined happiness as activity that accords with the specific nature of humanity. Pleasure accompanies such activity but is not its chief aim. Happiness results from the unique human attribute of reason, functioning harmoniously with human faculties. Aristotle argued that virtues are essentially good habits and that to attain happiness one should develop two kinds of habits, namely, those of mental activity, such as knowledge, which leads to the highest human activity, contemplation; and those of practical action and emotion, such as courage.

2.3.4 Stoicism

The philosophy of Stoicism developed in about 300 BC during the Hellenic and Roman periods. According to the Stoics, nature is orderly and rational, and only a life led in harmony with nature can be good. However, the Stoic philosophers also agreed that because life is influenced by material circumstances, one should attempt to be as independent of such circumstances as possible. The practice of certain cardinal virtues, such as wisdom, courage, discretion and justice, enables one to achieve independence in the spirit of the Stoic motto: 'endure and renounce'. Therefore, the word 'stoic' has come to mean fortitude in the face of hardship.

2.3.5 Epicureanism

In the 4th and 3rd centuries BC, the Greek philosopher Epicurus developed a system of thought, later called Epicureanism, which identified the highest good with pleasure, especially intellectual pleasure. Like Stoicism, Epicureanism advocated a temperate and even an abstinent life devoted to meditative pursuits. The principal Roman advocate of Epicureanism was the philosopher Lucretius, who combined certain ideas derived from the cosmological doctrines of the Greek philosopher Democritus with others derived from the ethics of Epicurus. The Epicureans sought to achieve pleasure by maintaining a state of serenity, by eliminating all emotional disturbances. They considered religious beliefs and practices harmful because they preoccupy one with disturbing thoughts of death and the uncertainty of life after death. They also held that it is better to postpone immediate pleasure in order to obtain more secure and lasting satisfaction in the future. They therefore insisted that the good life must be regulated by self-discipline.

Within a broad area of agreement, the Epicurean and Stoic ethics are presented as opposites: if both factions sought contentment, they sought it in divergent directions. For example, nature led the Epicureans to pleasure, while it led the Stoics to virtue. According to the Stoics, the objective is to live in agreement with nature, which is the same as to live in accordance with virtue, since it is virtue to which nature leads us (Boardman *et al*, 2001:366–367). Generally, the Sophists were moral sceptics because their professional stance ruled out an absolute position. They were mostly teachers. The teaching of success was their main aim, and one of the philosophical expressions of this aim was that justice is in the interest of the strong, or 'might begets right'.

Stoicism and Epicureanism were the last movements in Greek ethics. Both of them manifested themselves as ways of attaining control over our response to living conditions on earth. While the Stoics regarded life lived in accordance with the processes of nature as good, they nevertheless distinguished certain harmful aspects of life. They believed that dependence upon the material conditions of life had to be avoided, and that by means of training and discipline the individual could attain spiritual independence. The Epicureans dedicated their lives to the pursuit of pleasure, but in such a way as to minimise pain. Desire in itself was downgraded because of the continuous cycle of 'desire, fulfilment, desire, fulfilment, desire'. The Epicureans identified pleasure more with tranquillity than with any positive emotional state.

2.4 Religious ethics

The ethical systems of early ages were applied to the aristocracy in Greece, as in other societies. For example, the same standards were not extended to non-Greeks, and the term for them, *barbaroi* (barbarians), acquired insulting status. As for slaves, the attitude toward them may be summed up in Aristotle's characterisation of a slave as a 'living tool'. Partly for these reasons, as the pagan religions crumbled, the contemporary philosophies did not gain any popular following. Much of the appeal of Christianity was its extension of moral citizenship to all – even to slaves.

Religions over the ages have contributed much to the modern, democratised form of ethics and normative behaviour, although that of Western civilization has had the largest impact. What is discussed in this section is not a comprehensive view, but covers some of the major religions, as well as atheist ethics.

2.4.1 Jewish ethics

Jewish ethics is positioned at the intersection of Judaism and the Western philosophy of ethics (refer to en.wikipedia.org/wiki/Jewish_ethics). The diverse literature of Jewish ethics primarily aims to answer a broad range of moral questions, and may therefore be classified as normative ethics. Jewish ethics is said to have originated with the Hebrew Bible (or Old Testament). Most of the subsequent Jewish ethical claims may be traced back to the written Torah, which essentially refers to the Pentateuch or first five books of the Bible.

Jewish ethics has developed many spin-offs, due in part to developments in modern ethics as well as to the formation of Jewish denominations. Overall, Judaism places heavy emphasis on family life. In traditional Judaism, the head of a Jewish family was the father. In more modern movements within Judaism, the mother and father are regarded as equal in all things. The family plays a central role, socially and in transmitting the traditions of the religion. Jewish families strive to maintain close, respectful family relationships, with care for both the elderly and young. Religious observance is an essential part of home life. The Talmud, a collection of ancient writings on Jewish law and tradition, counsels parents to teach their children a trade and survival skills, and children are asked to look after their parents.

Other important principles of Jewish ethics include the importance placed on chastity and monogamy (marriage to one person). Chastity before marriage is regarded as of the highest importance, and monogamy is deemed to be the ideal. Virtue is believed to flow from the recognition of God. Non-Jews are regarded as falling within the conformity of ethical considerations. The Torah proscribes practices such as adultery, incest and homosexuality. Prostitution is forbidden. Honesty is a prerequisite. Stealing, flattery, falsehood, perjury and false swearing and oppression are forbidden.

2.4.2 Hinduism

In ancient India, elements of religion, race and social and regional institutions were fused into one living whole, which has come to be known as the Hindu religion. In the development of Hinduism, primitive forms of religious thought, such as fetishism and magic, were practised in unison with higher forms, such as asceticism, mysticism and higher considerations of a religious nature. One of the oldest of the world's major religions, Hinduism, originated from the merger of the West-Brahman religion of Aryan immigrants from the Indus Valley, southern India and elsewhere.

One of the oldest schools of Hinduism is Vedanta, which is based on two propositions: human nature is divine and the aim of human life is to realise that human life is divine. Three documents, the Upanishads, Bhagavad-Gita and Brahma Sutra, form the basis of Vedanta. From these scriptures are drawn the ethical principles that guide Hindus (refer to www.boloji.com/hinduism/032.htm). Among these ethical principles, personal discipline, good conduct, self-inquiry and meditation are important. There are nine basic requirements for a Hindu:

- Belief in the divinity of Vedas, which is a large body of texts originating in ancient India. Vedas manifest the divine word in human speech.
- The Supreme Being is both immanent (personally present) and transcendent.
- The universe is an endless cycle of creation and preservation.
- Individuals create their own destiny by thoughts, deeds and words.
- Every soul evolves through a series of births and deaths until all karma (the sum of people's actions in one of their successive lives, which is believed to decide their fate in the next) have been resolved.
- Belief in the existence of divine beings in unseen worlds.
- The guidance of a master or guru is essential to follow the right path to know the Transcendent Absolute.
- No one religion teaches the 'only pathway' to salvation.

2.4.3 Early Greek religion

Greek religion did not have a single origin (see Boardman *et al*, 2001:250–268). The Greeks were an Indo-European people who settled in the Aegean basin. Therefore, they came into contact with many advanced civilizations of the ancient Near East. Elements from all of these sources contributed to the amalgamation. When a god bears a name, he can be interpreted with certainty: Zeus patēr ('father') is the equivalent of Roman Diespiter (Jupiter) and Indian Dyaus pitar, all descended from the Indo-European god in heaven. Boardman *et al* (2001:250) add that the attributes of certain lesser gods may be regarded as equivalent.

In the religion of early Greece, the community did not correspond to the modern idea of the church. In Greece, power in religious matters lay with those who had secular power, i.e. with the father in the household, with the king in early communities, with the magistrates in developed city-states or even with the citizen assembly. The only true religious professionals in Greece were the seers. As interpreters of the divine will, seers could come into conflict with generals and politicians and their secular plans. However, there was no religious organisation that could spread moral teaching, develop doctrine or impose orthodoxy.

In ancient Greece, it was always possible that a stranger at the door might turn out to be a god (refer to crowdog.net/hospitality.html). Hospitality toward strangers and travellers formed an important element of Greek stories and myths, teaching people what was expected of them. Strangers could expect to be given a comfortable place to sit, to receive food, to enjoy charming company and to be accepted into the host's activities.

The Greeks regarded hospitality to perfect strangers as important. The idea was that a person's status in life does not matter. A stranger could very well be a god or goddess in disguise. If a god was not treated with due respect – a respect that was due to everyone – the potential existed for punishment.

According to Pargeter (refer to jmm.aaa.net.au/articles/352.htm), the ancient Greeks were proud of their hospitality to strangers, although at first strangers were treated with reserve and were not granted any rights. Gradually, and from a religious point of view, they were placed under the protection of Zeus, and their rights were increasingly defined. Relationships with the gods were also based on reciprocity: offerings for their blessings – in other words, gift for gift.

Traditional Greek ethics teaches that there is no shame in interpersonal conflict or just retribution – they are fundamental parts of life. Also, by not harming one's enemies one harms one's friends, thereby breaking down the fundamental bonds of society. The counterbalance to this harsh system is the virtue of *xenia*, which is the custom of offering hospitality and protection to strangers (the opposite to xenophobia) and that of *oikos*, which includes a resident 'family' of family members as well as all of those who live in the house or its dependencies and who contribute to its wealth and survival. This includes slaves, illegitimate children, residents-in-law and adopted persons who serve as retainers (refer to www.princeton.edu/~aford/terms.html).

The virtue of self-restraint (*sôphrosunê*) was highly regarded in Greek ethics. To exercise this virtue, one must act in accordance with the principle of prudence and moderation. The call for moderation was also a feature of the famed oracle of Apollo at Delphi. Above the entrance to the temple at Delphi were inscribed the maxims 'nothing in excess' and 'know yourself'. The former is a statement of the doctrine of moderation, while the latter merely means 'know that you are only human'. The term suggests that life-long happiness can be obtained when people's philosophical needs are satisfied and includes the idea of enlightenment through harmonious living. Although the ideal has faded over time, it has been revived in modern times with the emphasis on learning to live within the scope of reason. Some of the other inscriptions at Delphi continue to have validity today:

Aid friends
Control anger
Shun unjust acts
Hold on to learning
Praise virtue
Accomplish your limit
When you err, repent
Consider the time
Accept old age.

2.4.4 Christian ethics

Ethics is often defined as a set of moral principles and the study of morality. Therefore, Christian ethics would be the principles derived from the Christian faith by which Christians act. It is understood that the Bible does not cover every situation faced; the known principles give the necessary guidelines. Early Christianity emphasised such virtues as asceticism, martyrdom, faith, mercy, forgiveness and non-erotic love, few of which had been considered important by the philosophers of classical Greece or Rome.

The basis of Christian ethics is summarised in the New Testament of the Bible by St Paul in his letter to the Colossians, 3:1–6:

> *Since you have been raised from death with Christ, strive towards things above, where Christ is seated at the right hand of God. Set your hearts on things above and not on earthly things, for you died and your life is now hidden with Christ in God. When Christ, who is your life, appears, you will also appear with him in glory. Therefore, eradicate whatever belongs to your earthly nature: sexual immorality, impurity, lust, evil desires and greed, which is idolatry. Because of such things the wrath of God is coming to those who are disobedient to him.*

Christians believe that the Bible contains all that is necessary to know about how humans should live their lives. However, the Bible does not explicitly cover every situation faced in life. Nevertheless, its principles give the standards by which humans should conduct themselves in those situations where there are no explicit instructions. It is in the latter case where Christian ethics comes in. By using the principles found in Scripture, Christians are able to determine the ethical course for a given situation. Other influences that shaped Christian ethics are described below.

Ethics of the Church Fathers

One of the major shaping forces in Christian ethics was the competition with Manichaeism, a rival doctrine of Persian origin, which held that good and evil (light and darkness) were opposite forces struggling for mastery. Manichaeism had a large following in the 3rd and 4th centuries AD. St Augustine, regarded as the founder of Christian theology, was originally a Manichaean but abandoned Manichaeism after being influenced by Platonic thought. After his conversion to Christianity in 387, Augustine sought to integrate the Platonic view with the Christian concept of goodness as an attribute of God and sin as Adam's fall, from the guilt of which a person is redeemed by God's mercy. However, the Manichaean belief in evil persisted, as may be seen in Augustine's conviction of the sinfulness of human nature. This attribute may have reflected his guilt over his youthful indiscretions and may account, in part, for the emphasis in early Christian doctrine on chastity and celibacy.

During the late Middle Ages, Aristotle's works, made available through texts and commentaries prepared by Arab scholars, exerted a strong influence on European thinking. Because it emphasised empirical knowledge as opposed to revelation, Aristotelianism threatened the intellectual authority of the

Church. St Thomas Aquinas succeeded in reconciling Aristotelianism with the authority of the Church by acknowledging the truth of sense experience but holding it to be complementary to the truth of faith. Therefore, the intellectual authority of Aristotle was made to serve the authority of the Church, and Aristotelian logic was used to support the Augustinian concepts of original sin and redemption through divine grace.

Ethics and penance

As the medieval Church grew more powerful, a juridical system of ethics evolved, apportioning punishment for sin and reward for virtue in life after death. The most important virtues were humility, benevolence and obedience. Goodness of spirit was indispensable to morality. All actions, both good and bad, were graded by the Church, and a system of temporal penance was instituted as atonement for sins.

Ethics after the Reformation

The influence of Christian ethical beliefs and practices diminished during the Renaissance. The Protestant Reformation caused a widespread return to basic principles in the Christian tradition, changing the emphasis on certain ideas and introducing new ones. Martin Luther held that goodness of spirit is the essence of Christian piety. Moral conduct, or good works, is required of the Christian, but justification, or salvation, comes by faith alone. John Calvin accepted the theological doctrine that salvation is by faith alone and also upheld the Augustinian doctrine of original sin.

In general, during the Reformation, individual responsibility was considered more important than obedience to authority or tradition. This change of emphasis, which indirectly led to the development of modern secular ethics, is found in the *De Jure Belli ac Pacis* (On the Law of War and Peace, 1625) by the Dutch theologian and statesman, Hugo Grotius. Although the work adheres to some of the doctrines of St Thomas Aquinas, it deals with people's political and civil duties in the spirit of ancient Roman law. Grotius argued that natural law is a part of divine law and is based on human nature, which exhibits a desire for peaceful association with others and a tendency to follow general principles in conduct. Therefore, society itself is properly based on natural law.

2.4.5 Islamic ethics

The foundational source of the codification of Islamic ethics was the Muslim understanding and interpretations of the Qur'an and practices of the Prophet Muhammad (en.wikipedia.org/wiki/Islamic_ethics, 27 May 2009). Its constant meaning has been in active submission to Allah. The Qur'an defines and sets the standards of social and moral values for Muslims. A lengthy passage in the Qur'an represents the fullest statement of the code of conduct every Muslim has to follow. These resemble the Ten Commandments in the Bible.

The significance of a moral code and ethics in Islamic Shariah (both Muslim or Islamic criminal and civil law, as well as regulating personal and moral individual conduct) should be understood by the fact that there is so much text in the Qur'an and Sunnah (the fast that the Holy Prophet observed and urged his followers to observe) that if all of it were to be collected, it would create a large number of voluminous books. In summary, the Qur'an and the teachings of Muhammad cover the widest range of ethics. These cover the fields of:

- Environmentalism, which involves the use of natural capital;
- Humanism, including democratic participation, freedom of expression, and human rights;
- Medical ethics, including ethical standards of physicians, matters concerning drugs, medical peer review and neuro-ethics;
- Military ethics, including the law of treaties, the treatment of diplomats, hostages and prisoners of war, the right of asylum, conduct on the battlefield, protection of women, children and non-combatant civilians, contacts across the lines of battle, the use of poisonous weapons and devastation of enemy territory;
- Peace and justice. Peace is a basic concept in Islam. The Arabic word Islam may be translated as 'submission'. It comes from the term *aslama*, which means 'to surrender' or 'to resign oneself'. The Arabic word *salaam* (peace) has the same root as Islam. Some of the great Muslim scholars have stated, with reference to what Muhammad is reported to have said: 'Not one of you believes until he loves for his brother what he loves for himself', that the words 'for his brother' means every person, irrespective of faith;
- Public accountability, including an obligation to expose, to explain and to justify public actions and reactions;
- Welfare. Early Islamic law introduced the concepts of welfare and pension as forms of charity. The taxes collected in the treasury of

an Islamic government were used to provide income for the needy, including the poor, elderly, orphans, widows and the disabled.

2.4.6 Ethical atheism

Atheism is the doctrine of no god. It should be contrasted with agnosticism, which does not deny that God exists but rather denies that we actually know whether or not there is a supreme deity. It is interesting to note that the most significant argument offered in defence of atheism is a moral argument.

In essence, atheism involves disbelief in God. So, in principle, atheists may hold a range of ethical beliefs, from various forms of secular moral objectivism to moral nihilism (refer to www.investigatingatheism.info/morality.html). Certain scholars, such as Dawkins, Dennet and Harris strongly deny that atheism must lead to moral nihilism (rejection of all beliefs and values) and support the humanist project associated with the Enlightenment, the great flowering of rational and scientific thought that took place in Europe during the 17th and 18th centuries, which claims a secular autonomous ethics. There remains a suspicion, however, that atheism must unavoidably lead to immorality, and atheists devote a considerable amount of their time to addressing this charge.

2.5 Secular ethical philosophies

In 1651, Thomas Hobbes, in his book *Leviathan*, assigned major importance to organised society and political power. He held that human life 'in the state of nature' (apart from and before the institution of the civil state) 'is solitary, poor, nasty, brutish and short', and that it is a 'war of all against all'. As a result, people seek security by entering into a social contract in which each person's original power is yielded to a sovereign who regulates conduct. Therefore, one of the modern concepts of the role of politics in society was given greater emphasis.

This conservative position in politics assumes that human beings are evil and need a strong state to control them. However, Hobbes argued that if a sovereign does not provide security and order and is overthrown by the people, they revert to the state of nature and may then make a new contract. Hobbes's doctrine concerning the state and the social contract influenced the thought of John Locke. However, in his *Two Treatises of Civil Government* (1690) Locke maintained that the purpose of the social contract is to reduce the absolute power of authority and to promote individual liberty.

2.5.1 Ethics and geometrical order

Human reason is the criterion of right conduct in the system developed by Baruch Spinoza. In his *Ethica Ordine Geometrico Demonstrata* (Ethics Demonstrated with Geometrical Order, 1677), Spinoza deduced ethics from psychology and psychology from metaphysics. He held that all things are morally neutral from the point of view of eternity; only human needs and interests determine good and evil, or right and wrong. Whatever aids humanity's knowledge of nature, or is consonant with human reason, is acknowledged as good. Since it is reasonable to suppose that whatever all people have in common is best for everyone, the good that people should seek for others is the good they desire for themselves. Also, reason is needed in order to keep the passions in check and to achieve pleasure and happiness by avoiding pain. According to Spinoza, the highest human state is the 'intellectual love of God' derived from intuitive understanding, a faculty higher than ordinary reason. By the proper use of this faculty, a person may contemplate the entire mental and physical universe and view it as comprising an infinite substance, which he terms 'God'.

2.5.2 Newton's laws

Most major scientific discoveries have affected ethics. The discoveries of Isaac Newton in the 17th century provide some of the earliest examples of such an effect. Newton's laws were generally regarded as evidence of a divine order that is rational. Contemporary thinking in this regard was expressed concisely by Alexander Pope in the line, 'God said, let Newton be! And all was light'. Newton's discoveries caused philosophers to gain confidence in an ethical system as rational and orderly as nature was assumed to be.

2.5.3 Utilitarianism

In everyday usage, the term 'utilitarian' refers to a somewhat narrow economic or pragmatic viewpoint. However, ethical utilitarianism is much broader. Utilitarianism is the idea that the moral worth of an action is determined solely by its contribution to overall utility, i.e. its contribution to happiness and pleasure as summed among all people (refer to en.wikipedia.org/wiki/Utilitarianism). Hence it is a form of consequentialism. This means that the outcome determines the moral worth of an action. Utility, which means the good to be maximised, has been defined by various scholars as happiness or pleasure, as against suffering or pain, although it is also defined as the satisfaction of preferences, and may be described as a life stance, in which happiness or pleasure is of ultimate importance.

Utilitarianism is described by the phrase 'the greatest good for the greatest number of people', and is also known as 'the greatest-happiness principle'. Therefore, it can be characterised as a quantitative and reductionist approach to ethics. It can be contrasted with deontological ethics (which does not regard the consequences of an act as the sole determinant of its moral worth) and virtue ethics (which focuses on character), as well as with other varieties of consequentialism. Adherents of these opposing views have extensively criticised the utilitarian view, but utilitarians have been similarly critical of other schools of thought. As with any ethical theory, the applications of utilitarianism are heavily dependent on the moral agent's full range of wisdom, experience, social skills and life skills.

Utilitarianism has been used as an argument for many different political views. For example, in his essay *On Liberty*, as well as in other works, John Stuart Mill argues that utilitarianism requires that political arrangements satisfy the 'liberty principle' (or 'harm principle'), according to which the only purpose for which power can be rightfully exercised over any member of a civilised community against his or her will is to prevent harm to others. Prevention of self-harm by other persons was considered expressly forbidden. Instead, Mill states that only *persuasion* can rightfully be used to prevent self-harm. Others, such as Ludwig von Mises, advocated libertarianism using utilitarian arguments. Likewise, some Marxist philosophers have used utilitarianism as arguments for communism and socialism.

2.5.4 Evolutionary ethics

Evolutionary ethics tries to bridge the gap between philosophy and the natural sciences by arguing that natural selection has instilled in human beings a moral sense – a disposition to be good (refer to www.iep.utm.edu/e/evol-eth.htm). If this were to be true, morality could be understood as a phenomenon that arises automatically during the evolution of sociable, intelligent beings and not, as theologians or philosophers may argue, as the result of divine revelation or the application of our rational faculties. Morality would be interpreted as a useful adaptation that increases the fitness of its holders by providing a selective advantage. This is the view of the biologist Edward O. Wilson, who believes that scientists and humans should consider together the possibility that the time has come for ethics to be removed from philosophers and 'biologised'. Therefore, the challenge for evolutionary biologists is to define goodness in terms of evolutionary theory and then explain why humans ought to be good.

The biologisation of ethics began with Charles Darwin's *The Descent of Man* (1871), in which he applied his ideas about the evolutionary development of human beings. Darwin held that humans descended from a less highly organised form. His main difficulty in this explanation was the moral qualities of humans. Because of this, he devoted a chapter in the book to an evolutionary explanation of moral senses, which he argued developed in two main steps

Firstly, human morality is based in the social instincts, i.e. sociability is a trait whose biological origins can be traced back to the time birds devised brooding, hatching and caring for their offspring. To render beings able to fulfil parental responsibilities required social mechanisms unnecessary at earlier stages of evolutionary history. For example, neither amoebae (which reproduce by division) nor frogs (which leave their tadpole offspring to fend for themselves) need to have the social instincts of birds. In addition to facilitating the raising of offspring, social instincts counterbalanced inherent aggression. As a result it became possible to distinguish between 'them' and 'us' and to aim aggression towards those who did not belong to one's family.

Secondly, with the development of intellectual faculties, human beings were able to reflect on past actions and motives and to approve or disapprove of others as well as of themselves. This led to the development of a conscience, which became 'the supreme judge and monitor' of all actions. In line with utilitarianism, Darwin believed that the greatest-happiness principle would eventually be regarded as a standard for right and wrong by social beings with highly evolved intellectual capacities and a conscience.

Based on these claims, Darwin was probably not able to answer the two essential questions in ethics: how can we distinguish between good and evil?; and why should we be good? He accepts the greatest-happiness principle as a standard of right and wrong. Therefore, an action may be judged as good if it improves the greatest happiness of the greatest number, by either increasing pleasure or decreasing pain. The second question does not pose itself for Darwin with any urgency. Darwin would in all probability state that humans are biologically inclined to be sympathetic, altruistic and moral because this proved to be an advantage in the struggle for existence.

An important defender of evolutionary ethics, Herbert Spencer, created the theory of Social Darwinism. His theory can be summarised in three steps.

Firstly, Spencer believed in the theory of hedonistic utilitarianism. In his view, gaining pleasure and avoiding pain directs all human action, and moral good can therefore be equated with facilitating human pleasure. Secondly, pleasure can be obtained in two ways: by satisfying self-regarding impulses, and by satisfying other-regarding impulses, for example, eating one's favourite food and giving food to others are both pleasurable experiences for humans. Thirdly, mutual cooperation between humans is required to coordinate self- and other-regarding impulses, which is why humans develop principles of equity to bring altruistic and egotistic traits into balance.

Spencer did not become known for his theory of mutual cooperation. Quite the reverse: his account of Social Darwinism is highly contentious because it may be understood as an apology for systems of tyranny and oppression, such as National Socialism (Nazism) in Germany. Spencer elevated alleged biological facts, such as the struggle for existence, natural selection and survival of the fittest, to prescriptions for moral conduct. He held that to aid the bad in multiplying was the same as maliciously providing a multitude of enemies for our descendants.

It is interesting to pursue what answers Spencer could give to the two most essential questions in ethics: how can we distinguish between good and evil, and why should we be good? His answer to the first question is identical to that of Darwin, as Spencer also supported hedonistic utilitarianism. However, his answer to question two is untenable. He alleged that evolution equalled progress for the better (in the moral sense of the word) and that anything that supported evolutionary forces would therefore be good. The reasoning was that nature shows us what is good by moving towards it, and therefore evolution is a process that in itself generates value. If evolution advances the moral good, we ought to support it out of self-interest. Spencer identified moral good with universal human pleasure and happiness. If the evolutionary process directs us towards this universal pleasure, we have an egoistic reason for being moral, namely, that we want universal happiness. However, to equate development with moral progress for the better was a major value judgment, and most evolutionary theorists have dismissed the claim.

An important contribution to ethics was made by Immanuel Kant, in his *Grundlegung zur Metaphysik der Sitten* (Principles of the Metaphysics of Ethics, 1785). Kant argued that, no matter how intelligently one acts, the results of human actions are subject to accident and circumstance; the morality of an act must not be judged by its consequence, but only by its motivation.

Intention alone is good, for it leads a person to act, not from inclination, but from duty, which is based on a general principle that is right in itself. As the ultimate moral principle, Kant restates the golden rule in logical form: 'Act as if the principle on which your action is based was to become by your will a universal law of nature.' This rule is called the *categorical imperative*, because it is unqualified and a command. Kant further insists that one must treat all others as 'in every case as an end, never as a means only'.

In opposition to the concept of ruthless and unremitting struggle as the basic law of nature, some scholars presented studies of animal behaviour in nature demonstrating mutual aid. They asserted that the survival of species is furthered by mutual aid and that humans have attained primacy among animals in the course of evolution through their capacity for cooperation. The Russian Kropotkin's belief that governments are based on force and that if they are eliminated the cooperative instincts of people would spontaneously lead to a cooperative order, actually advocated anarchy.

Anthropologists applied evolutionary principles to the study of human societies and cultures. These studies re-emphasised the different concepts of right and wrong held by different societies. Therefore, it was believed that most such concepts added a relative rather than universal validity.

2.5.5 Hegelian ethics

In his *Grundlinien der Philosophie des Rechts* (Foundation of the Philosophy of Right, 1821), Georg Friedrich Hegel accepted Kant's categorical imperative (see above), but he included it in a universal evolutionary theory in which all history is regarded as a series of stages leading toward the manifestation of a fundamental reality that is both spiritual and rational. Therefore, morality is not the result of a social contract, but a natural growth arising in the family and finally culminating, historically, in the Prussian state of his time. He held that the history of the world constituted the discipline of the uncontrolled natural will, bringing it into conformity to a universal principle and conferring subjective freedom.

The Danish philosopher Søren Kierkegaard strongly responded to Hegel's system *In Either/Or* (1843), he expressed his most important ethical concern, namely, the problem of choice. He believed that philosophical systems, such as that of Hegel, obscure this crucial problem by making it seem an objective matter capable of a universal solution, rather than a subjective one that each person has to confront individually. Kierkegaard's own choice was to live within the framework of Christian ethics. His emphasis on the necessity of choice influenced several philosophers associated with the movement called existentialism (from existence), as well as a number of Christian and Jewish philosophers. Existentialism emphasises that human beings are responsible for their own actions and free to choose their development and destiny.

2.6 Psychoanalysis and behaviourism

Modern ethics has been greatly influenced by the psychoanalysis of Sigmund Freud and his followers and the behaviourist doctrines based on the conditioned-reflex discoveries of Ivan Pavlov. Freud attributed the good and evil in each individual to the struggle between the drive of the instinctive self to satisfy all its desires and the necessity of the social self to control or repress most of these impulses in order for the individual to function in society. Although Freud's influence has not been assimilated completely into ethical thinking, Freudian depth psychology has shown that guilt, often sexual, underlies much thinking about good and evil.

Behaviourism, through the observation of animal behaviour, strengthened beliefs in the power to change human nature by arranging conditions favourable to the desired changes. In the 1920s, behaviourism was broadly accepted in the USA, principally in theories of paediatrics, and infant training and education in general. However, one of the greatest influences was on thinking in the former USSR (Union of Soviet Socialist Republics, or Soviet Union). There, the so-called new Soviet citizen was developed according to behaviourist principles through the conditioning power of the rigidly controlled Soviet society. Soviet ethics defined 'good' as whatever was favourable to the state and bad as everything opposed to it.

In his late 19th century and early 20th century writings, William James anticipated Freud and Pavlov to a certain extent. James was the founder of *pragmatism*, which maintains that the value of ideas is determined by their consequences. His greatest contribution to ethical theory lies in his insistence on the importance of interrelationships, in ideas as in other phenomena.

By the 1950s, psychoanalytic theory and behaviourism had become the most influential schools of thought in psychology. However, many psychologists found these theoretical orientations unappealing (refer to psychology.about.com/od/historyofpsychology/a/hist_humanistic.htm). The main charge made against both schools was that they were dehumanising. Both theories were criticised because they suggested that people are not masters of their own destinies. Above all, both schools failed to recognise the unique qualities of *human* behaviour.

From the 1950s, the diverse opposition to psychoanalytic theory and behaviourism blended into a loose alliance that eventually became a new school of thought called *humanism*, a theoretical orientation that emphasises the unique qualities of humans, especially their freedom and their potential for personal growth. However, humanistic theory was often seen as too subjective. It was argued that the importance of individual experience makes it difficult to study and measure human phenomena objectively. We are able to rely only upon the individual's own assessment of their experience. Also, observation is unverifiable; there is no accurate way of measuring or of quantifying these qualities.

2.7 Contemporary trends

The philosopher Bertrand Russell has influenced ethical thinking in recent decades. He held that moral judgments express individual desires or accepted habits. In his view, both the ascetic saint and the detached sage are poor human models because they are incomplete human beings. Complete human beings participate fully in the life of society and express all of their nature. Some impulses must be checked in the interests of society, and others in the interest of individual development, but it is the person's relatively unimpeded natural growth and self-realisation that makes for the good life and harmonious society.

A number of 20th-century philosophers, such as Graves, Beck and Cowan, some of whom have adopted the theories of existentialism, have been concerned with the problem of individual ethical choice, as raised by Kierkegaard and Nietzsche. The orientation of some of these scholars is religious. Certain other modern philosophers do not accept any of the traditional religions. Martin Heidegger, for example, maintained that no God exists, although one may come into being in the future. Therefore, human beings are alone in the universe and have to make their ethical decisions with the constant awareness of death. The French philosopher Jean-Paul Sartre was an atheist who also emphasised the awareness of death. He maintained that people have an ethical responsibility to involve themselves in the social and political activities of their time.

Some other modern philosophers, such as John Dewey, have been concerned with ethical thought from the viewpoint of instrumentalism. In his view, the good is that which is chosen after reflecting upon both the means and the probable consequences of realising the good. Contemporary philosophical discussion in Britain and the USA is largely based on the writings of George Edward Moore, who argued that ethical terms are definable in terms of the word 'good', whereas 'good' is indefinable. This is so because goodness is a simple, unanalysable quality. Philosophers who disagree with Moore and believe that good is indeed definable are termed *naturalists*, while Moore is called an *intuitionist*. Both naturalists and intuitionists regard ethical sentences as descriptive of the world, and therefore true or false. Those philosophers who disagree with this belong to a third major school called *non-cognitive*, as against cognitive, and which refers to the mental processes of perception, memory, judgment, and reasoning, in contrast to emotional and volitional (voluntary) processes. An important branch of the non-cognitive school is *empiricism*, which questions the validity of ethical statements as compared with statements of fact or of logic. Some logical empiricists argue that ethical statements have only emotional or persuasive significance.

PRINCIPLES, VALUES AND NORMS PRESENTED IN THIS CHAPTER

Happiness or pleasure
Duty
Virtue or obligation
Natural human fulfilment
Public accountability
Prudence
Simplicity in speech, dress and food
Pleasure, especially intellectual pleasure
Self-control or temperance
Wisdom or knowledge
Justice
Fortitude
Self-discipline
Life lived according to the processes of nature

Tranquillity
Chastity
Honesty
Celibacy
Personal discipline
Self-inquiry
Controlling anger
Accomplishing one's limits
Humility
Benevolence
Obedience
Individual responsibility
Peace and justice
All people are equal
Social contract
Individual liberty
The good people seek for others is the good they desire for themselves
The moral worth of an action is determined by its outcome
Utility
The greatest good for the greatest number of people
Pleasure is obtained by satisfying self-regard and other-regard impulses
Mutual cooperation
Categorical imperative
Pragmatism
Self-realisation

Having studied this chapter, how would you now answer the question posed at the beginning?

Find an article or a report dealing with any aspect of religious ethics in any of the media and discuss the way in which it could influence the behaviour of public officials.

Chapter 3

Democratic basis of public ethics

IN THIS CHAPTER

After reading this chapter, you should be able to:

- define democracy;
- discuss the origins of democracy;
- discuss the emergence of the modern democratic state;
- outline the process of decolonisation;
- understand the phenomenon of the Third World.

Before studying this chapter, see if you can answer the following question:
How would you define *democracy*?

Viva! the Perpetual Revolution.

3.1 Introduction

As pointed out, the term 'democracy', on which the present South African Constitution is based, has over centuries developed many different and even opposing meanings. Few terms in the modern political vocabulary are used more often and more confusingly than democracy. During the so-called Cold War following the Second World War, the 'Western democracies' confronted the 'people's democracies' within the Soviet and Chinese orbits – each committed to the preservation and eventual triumph of what was believed to be the only true democratic dispensation for that particular society. In the West it was alleged that liberty and popular sovereignty were essential ingredients of democracy. On the other hand, the ruling party of the USSR declared that it was guided throughout by the Leninist principle of 'democratic centralism'. Soviet leader Josef Stalin declared that his 1936 constitution was the most democratic in the world.

3.2 Origins of democracy

The term 'democracy', which is so widely used and in such widely varying ways, could be said to have no real meaning. Ranney (1975:306–307) agrees that neither science nor logic can prove that any conception of democracy is the only correct one, i.e. one to which all people have to adhere if they are not to be regarded as irrational or immoral: 'The proper meaning of "democracy", like that of any other word, ultimately depends on convention: That is, its validity depends upon the degree to which it is generally understood and accepted.' Ranney (1975:307) does give a definition that he uses for the purposes of his book: '… a form of government organized in accordance with the principles of popular sovereignty, political equality, popular consultation, and majority rule.'

A full definition of the term 'democracy' would have to include its ethical, political and social elements as well as its development over time. So, if it cannot be defined in modern times, its true meaning may only be found in its origins and history rather than in its current usage.

3.2.1 Ancient Greece

In ancient Greece, from the earliest times, democracy had two distinct, yet related, usages – both in a specific, political and a general, sociological sense. The first of these is implied in the Greek roots of the word *demokrateo*, from *demos* ('the people') and *krateo* ('rule'). Therefore, in this sense democracy is a form of government in which political power is regularly exercised by the citizenry. In this connotation, we need to distinguish democracy from anarchy, which is an absence of government or the rule of everybody for themselves.

For many centuries, the history of the Greek city-states was a conflict between the forces of democracy and those of oligarchy (the rule of the few). The struggle between Athens and Sparta was virtually the struggle between two contrasting societies: the military despotism of Sparta and the democracy of Athens. These bloody attempts to find a form of government to replace the traditional aristocratic government of the city-states were inconclusive. By the 4th century BC, all participants were exhausted in both a military and a spiritual sense, and the city-state had virtually ceased to exist. However, the struggle was not without meaning or importance. It created the environment and stimulus for sophisticated discussions of the theory and practice of government – democratic, as well as oligarchic and aristocratic.

In the practice of Greek democratic government, widespread slavery was not only tolerated but was an essential feature. Democracy meant the direct participation of the mass of citizenry (not slaves) in the processes of government. Laws were made by vast popular assemblies, and officials were chosen by lot and served on a rotating basis. Lawsuits were decided by direct vote after bogus trials. All this meant that Greek citizens devoted a substantial amount of time to public affairs. Their commitment to personal involvement in public affairs was so strong that they were unable to imagine anything resembling representative government.

From the beginning, then, democracy meant more than simply a form of government. It was realised that governmental institutions reflect and shape communities. Therefore, we can say that democracy is a way of life as well as an ordering of public offices. In these terms, the democratic ideal is a community of free and equal citizens, a community in which the worth of each individual is recognised and cherished, and a community unmarked by special privilege of birth, wealth or status.

3.2.2 Ancient Rome

The Romans were more interested in political practice than theory and were therefore able to develop institutions capable of solving many of the problems of democracy that had mystified the Greeks. In that sense, the contribution of Roman lawyers and magistrates has arguably been more significant and more enduring than that of the Greek philosophers as far as the operation of democratic institutions is concerned. The Romans viewed citizenship as a matter of legal rights and duties, rather than active participation in public affairs.

For the first time, order and unity over large areas were achieved in ways that may be viewed as compatible with the ideals of democracy. In the pragmatic and complex evolving constitution of the Roman republic, a degree of political democracy was combined with monarchical and aristocratic elements to such an extent as to ensure a continuing popular voice in the conduct of Roman affairs. A core system of checks and balances, including the concept of the separation of powers, are found in this constitution. These elements, together with the Roman system of law guaranteeing uniform rights and equal treatment, form the bases of democratic government down to the present day.

3.2.3 The Middle Ages

For around a thousand years after the fall of Rome in AD 410, little remained of democracy, either as a form of government or as a social ideal. The collapse of the Roman world order was followed by centuries of rule by barbarian chieftains in the West and by the splendour of imperial Byzantium in the East. In Western Europe order was slowly but surely restored to larger and larger areas under the rule of the Roman Catholic Church, the Holy Roman Empire and the emerging national monarchies.

Ultimately, based on a belief in the essentially hierarchical structure of the universe and everything within it, the institutions of the Middle Ages were infused with the notions of superiority and inferiority. Privilege of any kind was not regarded as an abuse but rather as the organising principle of government and the community. Periodic uprisings of the 'lower orders' (notably the peasantry) indicated continuing discontent. However, such uprisings did not demonstrate important or widespread democratic sentiments among any stratum of the population of any European country during the Middle Ages.

The idea of the rule of law was kept alive during this period. It was cultivated by the Roman Catholic Church and found emphasis through the rediscovery of Roman law. Also, the increasing power of national monarchs met with a corresponding rise of opposition groups within every country. An example of the latter was the aristocratic Magna Carta in England in 1215, which to this day serves as the basis of British constitutional law and is one of the cornerstones of Western democratic ideology. The signing of the Magna Carta by King John could be regarded as the historical event that granted elected political representatives authority over such matters as public finance.

3.3 Emergence of the modern democratic state

Until the 1790s, the word 'democracy' remained a technical term, a tool to be utilised by experts such as political analysts. This was the case in Western Europe and its overseas possessions. Although the history of developing modern democracy may be traced as far back as the 16th century, until the era of the American Revolution there was no real possibility of establishing long-term democratic institutions on anything more than a local scale. The circumstances were also not conducive to the actual democratisation of any community larger than a village or perhaps a city.

In Europe prior to the 18th century, three main developments provided the foundations of what were to become thriving democracies. These were the ideals of the Renaissance, the theory and practice of Protestant Christianity and the rise and rapid strengthening of a middle class. Although not in themselves democratic movements, the Renaissance and Protestant Reformation contributed to the breaking-down of the hierarchical world of the Middle Ages, and both tended to enhance the importance and the recognised value of the individual human being.

The emergence in Western Europe of a dynamic and an increasingly powerful middle class, detached from the traditional ordering of the community, probably provided the most important resolution of traditional institutional loyalties and patterns. Until the emergence of the working class as a political force in the mid-19th century, the middle class (the *bourgeoisie* of Marxist doctrine) bore the brunt of the struggle against privilege and who fought for the extension of voting rights in Western Europe.

It is believed that the modern democratic state emerged in England during the 17th century. In the long struggle between Parliament and the Stuart monarchy, all the basic ideas of both political and social democracy were fully and vigorously expressed for the first time in modern history. By the end of the 17th century, after the civil war of 1640–48 and the bloodless revolution of 1688–89, the country was set on the course that two centuries later would bring the people to their democratic aspirations. Although the institution of monarchy remains to the present day, except for an eleven-year period of republican government from 1649 to 1660, the principles of government by consent, of representation and of the constitutional rule of law had been established.

3.3.1 The American and French Revolutions

The democratic and constitutional principles that had been expressed by John Locke and other Englishmen during the 17th century found greater acceptance in the New World. The colonists of America, freed from the burden of tradition and ancient privilege, were able to establish institutions capable of realising their ideals of liberty and equality. Guided by both the English tradition of constitutionalism, as well as more radical ideas, they exercised their freedom to establish a constitutional order based on the belief that everyone is born equal.

A constitution is a nation's basic rules for governing itself, defined by Ranney (1975:263) as '… the whole body of fundamental rules, written and unwritten, legal and extralegal, according to which a particular government operates'. The American colonists used their freedom to create a constitutional order based on the belief 'that all men are created equal, that they are endowed by the Creator with certain unalienable rights, that among these are life, liberty, and the pursuit of happiness' (see Ranney, 1975:523). Conversely, constitutionalism is the doctrine that the power of government should be limited so those human rights, such as free speech, free press, rule of law, due process and security of person, that are formally, and in fact, protected from contravention by either public officials or private individuals (Ranney, 1975:263–264).

Although the American Constitution did not contain all of the elements of democracy as it is understood today – it recognised and condoned the existence of slavery, and excluded many men and women from voting – America nonetheless at the end of the 18th century stood as a leading example of the peculiar modern phenomenon called the democratic state.

The enthusiasm of the French revolutionaries was fed by the American example. Their declaration of rights surpassed the American model as an expression of a fervent faith in democracy. According to this conception, the source of all sovereignty lies fundamentally in the nation. No body, no individual may exercise authority that does not proceed directly from the constitution. Liberty consists in the power to do anything that does not injure others, and law is the expression of the general will.

The process of industrialisation and consequent urbanisation, as well as the establishment of national states, resulted in a change in both local and national systems of government (Gildenhuys, 1993:52). This resulted in the emergence of representative democracy. The key principle of this form of democracy is the concept of political responsibility and accountability of the people's elected representatives, instead of direct participation by the individual citizen. The political responsibility and accountability of the elected political representatives guarantee that they will govern in the interest of the individual citizen and not in the exclusive interest of some defined groups, in the exclusive interests of the government only or in the personal interests of the political representatives themselves.

Representative government is based, firstly, on the principle of division of labour between the elected political representatives and the citizens, secondly, on the approachability of the political representatives by individual citizens and, thirdly, on the accountability of the political representatives. The origin of the principle of approachability may be found in the Magna Carta of 1215 and the slogan of 'no taxation without representation' of the American War of Independence.

As a consequence of the dominant position of the European nations as far as military and sea power were concerned, vast areas of the world were colonised by them. The resources of those colonies were exploited to the benefit of the colonial powers, which also used slave labour to advance their economies. These nations were therefore able, through industrialisation, to continue to dominate the world by military power. Many colonies, like America, gained their independence through civilian uprising, but many of the nations of the world remained colonised, some far into the 20th century.

In its Charter, the United Nations specified the basic rights of individuals. After the Second World War, it was decided that a universal declaration that specified the rights of individuals was necessary to give effect to the Charter's provisions. The Universal Declaration of Human Rights was adopted by the UN General Assembly on 10 December 1948 (see section 5.4 hereunder).

3.3.2 Decolonisation

Decolonisation has a long and interesting history, stretching back to ancient times. However, it was only after the Second World War that it gained momentum. In this process, the United Nations played a prominent role by granting de jure sovereign status to newly independent nations and by declaring that the principle of self-determination is of prime importance in the process of decolonisation. In the context of this book, the decolonisation of South Africa is important in order to gain an understanding of its present socio-political system of values.

Colonisation is the establishment of governance or authority through the creation of settlements by another country or jurisdiction. Decolonisation refers to the undoing of colonisation, i.e. the achievement after the Second World War of full or partial independence by a number of Western-administered colonies in Africa and Asia. Independence was gained by attaining full autonomy, integrating with the administering authority of another state or by establishing the status of 'free association'. Decolonisation was achieved through peaceful negotiation and/or armed struggle and revolt by indigenous populations (refer to en.wikipedia.org/wiki/Decolonisation).

In modern times, significant periods of decolonisation include the break-up of the Spanish empire in the 19th century, the gradual shrinking of the British and French empires after the Second World War, and the disintegration of the Union of Soviet Socialist Republics (USSR) after 1989.

The process of decolonisation frequently involves violence. In some cases there is a war of independence, often in the wake of a revolution. In many cases it follows a dynamic series of events where negotiations for independence fail and minor disturbances develop, which in turn develop in suppression by the police and military forces, escalating into violent revolts. This then leads to new rounds of negotiation until independence is finally gained. The actions of the indigenous population may be largely non-violent, as in the movement for Indian independence led by Mahatma Gandhi. In such cases, the violence comes mostly from occupying forces or from forces representing minorities who feel threatened by potential independence.

It is often difficult to achieve independence without the practical support and encouragement of one or more external parties. There are various reasons for such support: nations of the same ethnic or religious stock may sympathise with oppressed groups, or a prominent nation may attempt to destabilise a colony to weaken a rival or an enemy colonising power to promote its own sphere of influence; an example of this was British support for the Haitian revolution against France during the 18th century.

After the First World War there was a collective effort to advance the cause of independence through the newly created League of Nations. The intention was to prepare colonised nations for self-government, and a number of mandates were created (for example, Namibia, Lebanon and Palestine). These efforts were continued by the United Nations with the creation of a number of so-called trust territories to adjust control of former colonies and mandated territories administered by nations defeated in the Second World War.

After the Second World War, beginning with the granting of independence to India and Pakistan in the late 1940s, decolonisation by the Western powers gained momentum until even small nations such as Lesotho in Africa and the Cook Islands in the Pacific gained full political independence. One of the last phases of decolonisation involved the granting of independence to the various territories colonised by Portugal, such as Angola (1975), Mozambique (1975) and Macau (1999).

3.3.3 Emergence of the Third World

Decolonisation gained momentum after the Second World War, but this drive began even before 1939. In 1931, the Statute of Westminster granted virtually full independence to Canada, New Zealand, Newfoundland, the Irish Free State, the Commonwealth of Australia and the Union of South Africa, when it declared the British Parliament incapable of passing laws over these former colonies without their consent. In 1961, South Africa declared itself a republic and withdrew from the British Commonwealth.

The origin of the term 'Third World' is uncertain (refer to www.answers.com/topic/third-world), but during the Cold War it was applied to 'underdeveloped' (later termed developing) countries that belonged to neither the capitalist West nor the Soviet-dominated socialist bloc. The Third World, mostly former colonies, was politically non-aligned and included the poor counties of Africa, Asia and Latin America. On economic and developmental grounds it was also referred to as the South, in contrast to the largely industrialised North.

The technology of the South was far less advanced than that of the North, and the countries of the South were generally characterised as poor, with economies distorted by their almost total exclusion from international trade and by their dependence on export of primary goods, such as iron ore, coal and agricultural produce. By and large, Third World countries also experienced high rates of population growth, high occurrence of disease, and unstable government.

Numerically, the Third World dominates the United Nations, but the group is widely diverse as far as ideology and economic progress are concerned. Some oil-rich nations such as Kuwait and Libya and newly industrialised states such as Taiwan and South Korea have little in common with poor nations such as Haiti and Sudan. To add to the economic and political problems, many Third World countries are vulnerable to natural calamities, civil unrest, corrupt and dictatorial governments and shortages of basic commodities.

The international community, led by the United Nations and its agencies, actively extends aid, support and expertise to countries in need. International co-operation and investment in various fields is also aimed at the overall development of the poor nations. However, issues such as reform of the world's economic order, ongoing political and civil unrest and systemic corruption in many third World countries need to be addressed.

3.4 Modern approaches to decolonisation

Although the term 'decolonisation' is not altogether acceptable among international development donors today, the emerging emphasis on projects to promote democracy, governance and human rights, and to promote institution-building and a human rights-based approach to development, shares the objective of achieving final decolonisation.

In some countries, the human rights challenges are to empower women and reverse the legacy of converting people to certain beliefs or opinions that promoted patriarchy, and to empower individuals and civil society through changes in education systems that were set up by colonial governments to train obedient servants of colonial regimes.

The effects of the economic recession of 2008–2009 were felt throughout the world. As far as South Africa is concerned, the effects of the global recession did not have such a devastating impact on its economy. However, Chuma observed that the country was starting to feel the crunch, especially in its manufacturing and export sectors. Other countries in the region felt the impact immediately, which further retarded growth and development in those countries, especially as far as the eradication of poverty, and education, health and political reform are concerned (refer to www.twnafrica.org/index.php?option=com_content&view=article&id=84:globa).

PRINCIPLES, VALUES AND NORMS PRESENTED IN THIS CHAPTER

The origins of democracy
The emergence of the modern democratic state
Decolonisation
Phenomenon of the Third World
Majority rule
Public accountability
Moral and intelligence education
Empathy
Conscience
Self-control
Tolerance
Fairness
Respect
Altruism

Having studied this chapter, how would you now answer the question posed at the beginning?

Critically analyse the term 'democracy' as discussed in this chapter.

Chapter  4

Developing democratic principles

IN THIS CHAPTER

After reading this chapter, you will be able to:

- discuss developments in democracy during the 19th century;
- understand the democratic experiments of the 20th century;
- understand the Soviet model of democracy;
- understand the Chinese model of democracy;
- discuss the meaning of direct or participatory democracy;
- discuss the meaning of indirect or elitist democracy;
- explore agreement and disagreement on democratic models;
- outline early 21st-century thinking regarding democracy.

Before studying this chapter, see if you can answer the following question:
Does the democratic way of life have a long history?

Democratic Evolution in Practice.

4.1 Democracy in the 19th century

During the 19th century, many people were horrified and frightened by democracy. It is a fact of history that many men opposed democracy in the name of absolutism or of ancient privilege. Others had more liberal views. Their fear was that democratic government might in time become no less tyrannical and destructive of human freedom and creativity than other forms of government. They sensed that there may develop the 'tyranny of the majority'. They were obviously concerned to discover means of making democracy safe for the world. They accepted progressive democratisation as an inevitable, and even desirable, development, and aimed at warning against the perils involved and suggesting means of avoiding those perils.

Their achievement was that people were made aware of the problems involved. By the mid-20th century, it had become generally recognised that pure direct mass democracy was an unstable and explosive form of government. The need for constitutional restraints and checks and balances even in democratic governments are now generally accepted. However, the awakening of this realisation was a slow and difficult process.

4.2 Experiments in the 20th century

The first decades of the 20th century saw the most infantile enthusiasm for democracy in the Western world. It was believed by many that democratic rule had been so firmly established that it should form the basis of all future states. After the victory by the Allied powers in the First World War, it was believed that the world would be safe for democracy. The general acceptance of democracy corresponded to the dramatic spread of democratic institutions in many countries, such as Germany, Poland and even Russia (for a short period after the 1917 revolution). Also, democracy became more established in the older European states and in America. Many observers concluded that the world was about to enter a new and untroubled era of universal democracy.

By 1939, however, the dominance of democracy was no longer evident. This started in 1922 in Italy, when democracy was overthrown by the Fascists. In 1933 the democratic government in Germany was overthrown, and during the 1930s the democratic constitutions of Spain, Poland, Lithuania, Turkey, Bulgaria, Greece and Austria were demolished. By 1939, every newly established democracy of Europe had been destroyed. The commitment to democratic rule had been severely shaken.

In the belief that every abuse in a democratic government could be traced to some undemocratic element, reformers introduced so-called 'ultra-democratic' measures. The most important of these were female suffrage and the referendum. These measures were designed to narrow the gap between citizens and their political representatives. The days of trying to solve the problems of democracy by adopting the methods of direct democracy have now lapsed. In many cases they caused problems of their own. Proportional representation, for example, in Germany and France led to the over-representation of extremist splinter groups and made the orderly conduct of government almost impossible. It has become evident that democracy is not the simple, self-correcting system that had once been believed.

Many believe that democracy should not and cannot survive. However, after the Second World War the democracies had proved themselves able to meet a deadly global challenge and to mobilise the material and spiritual resources of a great number of people in defence of the democratic way of life. The cessation of hostilities led to a remarkable number of real democratic governments, even in the more remote areas of the world. Many of the latter fell back on monolithic political power and a totalitarian organisation of the community. They believed that the only way to achieve a community in which exploitation and inequality do not exist is through the hierarchy of a political party.

Whatever is evident from what governments of the early to later 20th century all over the world claimed as the model democracy, there was confusion and disagreement about what democracy really is (see Ranney, 1975:301–306). The most influential brand of democracy during the 20th century was the communist model, of which the Soviet Union and Chinese versions were the most prominent, while the non-communist models of democracy ranged from the direct or participatory to the indirect or elitist models.

4.2.1 Communist models

The Soviet model

The Soviet government's interpretation of the doctrines of Marx and Lenin maintained that only theirs, and those of the people's republics modelled on that of the Soviet Union, might legitimately be called democratic. They insisted that what Western countries such as Sweden and the USA called 'democratic' were merely false fronts raised by capitalists to conceal the realities of their exploitation of the masses.

The core of the Soviet concept was the conviction that true democracy is a regime within which government action advances the real interests and welfare of the masses, i.e. what was objectively good for the masses and not necessarily what the masses may want. That meant that democracy was a matter of what government does and not of how government decides what to do. It is government for the people and not necessarily government by the people.

However, the Soviet model of democracy does have a few notable procedural elements. The view was that the Communist Party is the vanguard of the proletariat. It was believed that the highly trained and dedicated proletarian elite of the party knew far better than did the masses what was best for them and how to achieve it. To permit freedom of organisation and expression for non- or anticommunist opponents of party policies would be undemocratic. It would allow capitalist exploiters, social fascists and other enemies of communism to impede and sabotage the party's programmes, which would mean sabotaging the welfare of the masses. Therefore, the regime's acceptance of only one party, suspension of most forms of dissent and single-candidate elections were the only truly democratic modes of conducting government.

Related to the 'vanguard' concept of the party's place in society was the principle of democratic centralism in the party's internal decision-making. Democratic centralism proclaimed full, fair, free and frank discussions of alternatives within the party before a decision was made, but demanded total and unwavering support of the policy by all once the party had made its choice. According to most Western students of the Soviet system at that time, democratic centralism meant that free discussion and dissent were confined strictly to certain matters selected by the party leaders. Those matters were limited to questions about the most effective way to carry out party policies, and did not include direct criticism of the policies themselves or of the leaders who made them.

The Soviet system included devices for discovering the reaction of the masses to party policies and for arousing mass approval and enthusiasm. However, although the welfare of the masses remained the proclaimed paramount end of the government, decisions on what measures would best achieve that end remained strictly the monopoly of the party vanguard.

The Chinese model

During the 1960s the Chinese government strongly criticised the Soviet Union for, according to them, deserting the true communist principles of

Marxism-Leninism, especially for accepting the principle of 'revisionism'. The Chinese model of communism was similar to the Soviet version, but there were differences in language and emphasis between the two systems. The most noteworthy was the Chinese communists' doctrine of the 'mass line', which meant the integration of the party's leadership with the physical power of the masses in order to build true communism. The mass line involved a two-way interaction of leadership by the party's cadres in farms, villages, cities and factories in order to mobilise, inspire and energise the masses to do what the party had decided had to be done, as well as the sensitivity of the party, through its cadres, to the masses' aspirations and feelings.

In its 1945 constitution, the Chinese Communist Party clarified the mass-line concept by describing a number of deviations from the mass line that all cadres were obliged to avoid. The first was defined as the incorrect practice of blindly following untutored popular demands because the party knows best. The other deviations were 'commandism', 'isolationism', bureaucratism' and 'warlordism', which all were forms of behaviour attributed to cadres and public officials who had become too far removed from, and out of feeling with, the masses.

The party, as the vanguard of the working class, exercised leadership as its major function in the mass-line process. The party controlled by leading and the masses controlled by participating, and within the vanguard theory the party could not have interests different from those of the masses. It was held that the masses were more contaminated by reactionary ideologies and counter-revolutionary elements. Chairman Mao implied that the ordinary Chinese had neither the duty to create the mass-line relationship nor the right to reject it. The masses could not turn against the vanguard because they could not reverse the tide of their own historical movement that created the vanguard.

4.2.2 Non-communist models

In non-communist models, there was no single model of democracy but rather several, of which not one pre-empted the label of democracy all for itself. These models shared specific areas of agreement, yet were sufficiently different to warrant discussion. The two most influential of these were the direct or participatory and the indirect or elitist models.

As indicated, the term 'democracy' was originally compounded from two Greek words: *demos*, meaning 'the people', and *krateo*, meaning 'ruling power'. Its original meaning was 'the government in which the ruling power resides in the people'. From the 5th century BC until the 20th century most people using the word referred to the government system of the city-state of Athens at the time of Pericles. Under that system, all important decisions were made directly by the *ekklisia*, the general face-to-face assembly of all the citizens. The two principal qualities of Athenian democracy were popular control of public decisions and maximum popular participation in making decisions and holding public office.

Most political theorists believe that this kind of direct popular participation in day-to-day government is impossible in modern nation-states, almost all of which have millions of people as apposed to perhaps 40 000 in Periclian Athens. However, some theorists argue that any idea of democracy settling for less than maximum direct popular participation cannot be a valid model of democracy. The moral goal of democracy, the basic purpose for which it exists, was and remains to develop the full human potential of each member of society. The only logical way to direct government structure to this goal is to encourage maximum participation of all the people in the making of those decisions, public or private, that affect their lives.

The way this can be done is to permit and encourage greater popular participation in smaller sub-governmental decision-making bodies, such as political parties, labour unions, corporations, schools and churches. In addition, a larger share of public power should be delegated to government units small enough to permit effective and meaningful mass participation in decision-making, particularly small municipalities and neighbourhoods within large cities.

Many other devices would also be needed, but the first and most important step is to recognise that **personal self-development** is the moral goal of democracy and that maximum direct popular participation is the chief means of achieving it. When people generally understand and accept these basic principles, they can proceed with the largely technical activities of developing new and better means for increasing popular participation.

Most social scientists agree that in almost no human organisation do all members participate all the time with equal energy, commitment and influence. In every organisation, a few members are more committed, more willing to work, more likely to take initiative and, as a result, to have more influence than the more passive majority. Social scientists usually call these more active and influential members the organisation's 'elite'.

Many theorists believe that the prevalence of influential elites in human groups does not mean that democracy is impossible. The essence of democracy lies not in the absence of elites but in popular control of the elites. In this model, control is exercised through the **competition** of elites for office and power, **popular selection** of the winners by the people in periodic elections, **limitations** of the power that any elite may exercise while in office, and the **removal** of incumbent elites whenever they fail to perform to the people's satisfaction, i.e. through the accountability to the people of the elite in power at the time.

To those theorists, a properly organised representative or indirect democracy is in principle just as democratic as the direct or participatory kind. Rather than wasting time and energy in hopeless searches for ways to bring about universal popular participation in modern governments, they hold that the focus should be on the more significant quest for ways of establishing effective popular control of such governments.

4.2.3 Agreement and disagreement

Outside the communist world, the term 'democracy' has different meanings. However, all is not sheer chaos and confusion, as a survey and comparison of different meanings reveals that they share areas of agreement, as well as areas of disagreement.

Areas of agreement

Almost all believe that democracy is at least a form of government, i.e. a particular way of arriving at government decisions. Further, they agree that a genuinely democratic government must have at least three characteristics:

- **Political equality:** In a democracy, each member of society must have the same legal and actual opportunity to participate in the political decision-making processes enjoyed by every other member. If certain people have more such opportunities than other members of society – for example, by being members of the only tolerated party – the favoured few are a 'ruling class'. Such regimes should be called *oligarchies* rather than democracies.
- **Governmental response to the popular will:** A democratic government does whatever the people want it to do and refrains from doing whatever they do not want it to do. In a democracy, the people – not the elite of party members, or business people or university professors – are the final judges of what is in their best interests. Democracy is government *by* the people.

- **Majority rule rather than minority rule:** When the people disagree among themselves about what government should do and a decision must be made, the democratic way to decide is by majority rule. All members of society should register their wishes (in an election or a referendum or by other democratically accepted methods), the results should be totalled, and public officials should be mandated to act in accordance with the wishes of the greater proportion of the people (the majority) rather than the wishes of the lesser proportion (the minority). Many non-communists believe that popular majorities in a true democracy must not adopt certain kinds of policies, but none argue that minority rule is more democratic than majority rule in determining which of the permissible policies government will follow.

Areas of disagreement

The main differences among non-communists about the proper meaning of democracy centre on two basic issues:

- **Limitations upon popular majorities:** Some non-communists believe that popular majorities in a democracy must not do certain things, such as abridge the rights of individuals. They argue that true democracy should have certain institutional machinery, such as judicial review, to restrain majorities from ignoring or stepping outside their proper limits. Others insist that any limitation upon popular majorities other than that imposed by the majorities themselves and removable by other majorities at any time means minority veto power and therefore minority rule.
- **Form of government:** Some non-communists believe that democracy should be regarded solely as a form of government, a method of making public decisions not directly concerned with the content of those decisions or with the purposes to which government power may be directed. However, others argue that the concept of democracy, even though it includes certain ways of making political decisions, includes other considerations as well, such as a certain kind of economic system or certain kinds of relations among the races. To them, democracy is more than simply a form of government. It is also a communal or personal way of life.

4.3 Into the 21st century

The 20th century has been criticised as a series of disasters in terms of its morality, and has been characterised by a pursuit of final solutions and, through colonisation, the imposition of a defined Western conceptualisation of ethics (see Raga, 2009).

The table below is a comparison of public sector ethics in the 20th century with envisaged public sector ethics for the 21st century:

Determinants – ruling elites	Determinants – authentic discourse among all who will be affected
Common ethical code – belief in final solutions	Constantly managing code(s) – based on continuous authentic discourse
Support guaranteed through coercion	Support guaranteed through consensus
Dissenters subject to punitive measures	Dissenters subject to punitive measures
Western (colonial) ethics	Ethics based on anthropological and sociological pluralism
Corporate accountability (amounts to non-accountability)	Personal accountability
Exercise of personal morality stifled and discouraged	Exercise of personal morality encouraged
Exercise of personal discretion discouraged	Exercise of discretion encouraged
Public interest nebulous, determined by governing elites	Public interests(s) disparate but relatively distinct, determined with all involved (authentic discourse), constantly redefined

It can be inferred from the above-mentioned examples that, in the 21st century and beyond, ethics can contribute neither to high-quality public service nor to a more equitable distribution of scarce resources. In 20th-century society and in government and administration, efforts were made to guarantee morality by legally binding ethical codes and legislation. This resulted in the destruction of democratic decision-making and innovative discretion. Sophisticated techniques of social engineering were employed to punish dissenters for insubordination and make people moral in order to guarantee moral behaviour. Ethical behaviour was defined in terms of whether or not public officials subjected themselves to the codes of conduct. This state of affairs has been referred to as the ethic of neutrality, whereby the public official was not expected to exercise her or his own discretion but was required to follow rules external to herself or himself.

The result of an absence of discretion in performing duties on behalf of the public is that personal accountability can hardly be claimed or apportioned. This situation lends itself to totalitarianism, which in turn results in inhumanity, reducing the human spirit to a mechanical entity without initiative, without creativity and without love or emotion. This mode of governing characterised the apartheid regime in South Africa prior to 1994. That government was characterised by public officials uncritically executing state edicts that amounted to injustice, and the failure or fear to make judgments based on basic human rights. Public officials acted as if void of personal values and masqueraded as obedient agents executing the directives of their superiors.

The fall of the Berlin Wall in 1989 marked the beginning of the end of many totalitarian regimes. Many countries gained their independence and opted for democratic government. Many adopted the Western democratic tenets of political participation, spontaneous organisation of groups and parties, free speech and publication, responsible criticism and the sharing of public power. Many of the countries that had gained their independence from colonial rule earlier in the 20th century, and which had opted for more socialist types of regimes, had to adapt. Apart from the civil wars that had marked the post-independence period, governments tended to become more totalitarian, with one-party regimes and life-long presidents.

One of the exceptions was South Africa, where a fully democratic government was only elected in the very late 20th century. The South African Constitution has been acclaimed as one of the most democratic constitutions on earth, and contains what is regarded as the full range of modern democratic principles. It was negotiated between rival parties after the end of a prolonged struggle for independence. Civil war did not break out, as was the case with some African nations after independence.

4.3.1 Ethics of democracy

As pointed out in other contexts, the word 'democracy' comes from the Greek *demos* (people) and *krateo* (rule), and means 'rule by the people' (refer to www.cooperativeindividualism.org/clancy-robert ethics-of-democracy.html). Ethics is the science of human duty; the science of right and a moral science. Ethics in democracy seems in some quarters to be only a point of view. The ethics of democracy refers to those considerations of morals and rights on which democracy has to be founded and according to which it has to be built to be right and just.

The equality of all people is the fundamental truth of democracy. This means that everyone is endowed with equal and inalienable rights – for example, the rights to 'life, liberty and the pursuit of happiness' as enshrined in the United States Declaration of Independence. No form of government has any right to compel individuals regarding their individual concerns. This is an invasion or an aggression and remains so whether or not the invader is a government and not an individual or a mob.

Individual rights are not initiated in government, but are merely recognised, or ought to be recognised, by government and made secure by government. People do not exist for government – governments exist for people. Whatever rights people have are inherent in them by reason of their very existence. People form themselves into communities to make life easier and more secure, and government is or should be merely the orderly conduct of community affairs.

The rights of government are delegated to it by individuals. Rights carry with them correlative duties. To say that all people have equal rights is the same as saying that each has a duty to respect the rights of all. This principle is expressed by what is known as the *Golden Rule*: 'Do unto others as you would have them do unto you.'

There are two classes of rights in human society: those pertaining to individuals and those pertaining to communities. Individual rights and duties are inherent and complete in individuals, for example every person has a right to live. Community rights and duties attach to the community as a whole. For example, the community as a whole has the right to the terms of land tenure and the expenditure of common income.

Self-government, as to individual rights, implies that individuals shall govern themselves, free from all government interference, provided that they respect the individual rights of other individuals. As to community rights, each individual shall have a voice, and the majority vote has to be taken as the corporate expression. However, even the majority vote cannot deprive individuals of their rights.

Individual liberty is the test of morality in democracy. Immorality, as between persons, consists in the imposition of one person's will upon another. Morality in democracy consists in the practical recognition of the absolute liberty of each, limited only by the equal liberty of all. Acceptance of these principles precludes, for example, the recognition by government of any type of slavery or that lead to virtual slavery. Government is therefore precluded from any monopoly that tends to restrict or to proscribe the equal rights of all to life, liberty and to the right to enjoy all the opportunities that life offers.

Clancy holds that human labour is the basis of economic research. At the economic level, labour is economically self-existent. The word 'labour' is a technical term descriptive of the human family, producing satisfactions for human desires. Wealth is labour in a tangible form, and when producers or workers exchange among themselves the wealth they have produced, they are exchanging one person's labour for that of another. In exchanging products of labour, humans are exchanging service for service and work for work.

Service for service is the condition of civilised life. It is only through some degree of interchange of service that humans can live civilised lives. This brings into play the democratic principle of the obligation of individuals and groups to render service to government and government to deliver service equally to every individual.

Exchange of trade or the rendering and acceptance of service, must be upon the basis of equal exchange. It is unjust to get without giving or to give without getting. No one may justly give or sell or exchange what is not their own. Whatever people produce or receive from others in exchange for what they have produced, is their rightful property. No individual or group, not even the government, has the right to deprive an individual of any part of what she or he owns or has produced.

An enduring structure of democracy can be built only upon these foundations of human rights.

PRINCIPLES, VALUES AND NORMS PRESENTED IN THIS CHAPTER

Constitutional restraints
Direct democracy
Model democracy
Direct or participatory democracy
Indirect or elitist democracy
Direct popular participation
Personal self-development
Political equality
Governmental equality
Majority rule rather than minority rule
Rule by all of the people
Protection of fundamental rights is a public duty
Self-defence against aggression is an individual right
Equality of rights of all people
Government rights delegated by the people
Equal and inalienable rights of life, liberty and pursuit of happiness, with equal rights for all
Majority vote is the corporate expression
The majority cannot deprive individuals of their rights
Everyone must own what they give
Nobody may deprive anybody of what they own or have produced

Having studied this chapter, how would you now answer the question posed at the beginning?
Write an essay of about 500 words on the way you and your friends would like democracy to develop in South Africa.

Chapter  5

Legal framework

IN THIS CHAPTER

After reading this chapter, you should be able to:

- define the term 'common law';
- define the term administrative law';
- explain the importance of the Universal Declaration of Human Rights;
- discuss the major ethical points in the South African Constitution;
- explain the main points in the South African Bill of Rights;
- understand the nature of cooperative government;
- understand the structure of the South African government;
- discuss the concept of core public business;
- explain the process of public policy-making;
- define the term 'public resources';
- understand the public budget;
- outline the nature of government goals and objectives;
- explain the process of public planning;
- outline the process of budgeting.

Before studying this chapter, see if you can answer the following question:
Is the Bill of Rights found in the South African Constitution unique to South Africa?

Power to the people to pay the bills.

5.1 Introduction

The legal framework within which a democracy functions is a result of the ethics of democracy. The Constitution is the supreme law of the South African democratic landscape. As the Constitution is written in broad terms, certain sets of legislation and policies have to be adopted to elucidate what it in fact signifies. Also, South Africa is one of the countries where common law principles form part of the body of law. The chapter does not go into any specific laws emanating from the Constitution, as this would take up too much space and would revolve around legal discussions. One of the democratic principles in this constitutional democracy is that all legislation and public action is subject to review by the Constitutional Court.

5.2 Common law

Common law refers to law and the corresponding legal system developed through decisions of courts and similar tribunals (called case law), rather than through legislative statute or executive action (refer to en.wikipedia.org/wiki/Common_law). Common law is law created by judges: a decision in a currently pending legal case depends on decisions in previous cases and affects the law to be applied in future cases. When there is no authoritative statement of the law, judges have the authority and duty to make law by, what is called, precedent.

The body of precedent is called 'common law' and it binds future decisions. In future cases, when parties disagree on what the law is, an idealised common law court will look at precedential decisions of relevant courts. When a similar dispute had been resolved in the past, the court will be bound to follow the reasoning used in the prior decision. This principle is known as *stare decisis*, which literally means 'to stand by that which is decided'. This is the principle that precedent decisions have to be followed by the courts (refer to www.lectlaw.com/def2/s065.htm).

As a rule, when a point has been settled by court decision, it forms a precedent from which courts may afterwards not depart. However, the doctrine of *stare decisis* cannot always be relied upon, because courts find it necessary to overrule cases that have been decided contrary to principle or in haste. This does not prevent re-examination and perhaps overruling of prior decisions. However, jurisprudential policy remains that applicable precedent must be followed even though the case, when considered anew, may be decided differently. This is based on the assumption that predictability, certainty and stability in the law are the major objectives of the legal system, which implies that the parties should be able to regulate their conduct and enter into relationships with reasonable assurance of the governing rules of law.

In practice, common law systems are considerably more complicated than the idealised system described above. A court's decisions are binding only in a particular jurisdiction, and even in a given jurisdiction some courts have more power than others. For example, in many jurisdictions decisions by appellate courts (courts of appeal) are binding on lower courts in the same jurisdiction and on future decisions of the same appellate court, but decisions of non-appellate courts have only non-binding, persuasive authority. Interactions between common law, constitutional law, statutory law and regulatory law also give rise to substantial complexity.

Common law systems form a legitimate and important part of South African law. In the case of *FS Masiya v Director of Public Prosecutions*, Case No CCT 54/06 of 10 May 2007, nothing unconstitutional was found in a common law judgment, which shows that common law judgments may be tested as to their constitutionality but need not necessarily be unconstitutional or be in conflict with the Constitution.

5.3 Administrative law

Administrative law is the body of law that governs the activities of administrative institutions of government. Institutional action may include rule-making, adjudication or enforcement of a specific regulatory agenda. Administrative law is regarded as a branch of public law. As a body of law, administrative law deals with the decision-making of administrative units of government, such as boards, commissions or tribunals, which are part of a national regulatory scheme in such areas as broadcasting, the environment, immigration, international trade, manufacturing, police, law, taxation and transport (refer to en.wikipedia.org/wiki/Administrative_law).

Most countries that follow the principles of common law (see section 5.1) have developed procedures for judicial review that limit the reviewability of decisions made by administrative law bodies. Section 33 of the South African Constitution, concerning administrative justice, provides that 'everyone has the right to administrative action that is lawful, reasonable, and procedurally fair' and that anyone whose rights have been adversely affected by administrative action has a right to be given written reasons. However, as Asimow (1996) has pointed out, those rights should be implemented through national legislation, and he argues that Parliament should adopt an administrative justice Act to limit and implement the section 33 rights (refer to papers.ssrn.com/sol3/papers.cfm?abstract_id=10406).

Although administrative decision-making bodies are often controlled by larger government units, their decisions may be reviewed by a court of general jurisdiction under principles of judicial review. Judicial review of administrative decisions differs from an appeal. When reviewing such a decision, the court will investigate only the method (procedure) through which the decision was reached and not the correctness of the decision itself, as in the case of an appeal. The scope of judicial review may also be limited to certain questions of fairness or whether the administrative action is *ultra vires* (unauthorised).

5.4 Universal Declaration of Human Rights

The Universal Declaration of Human Rights is a document adopted by the United Nations General Assembly in Paris on 10 December 1948 (refer to en.wikipedia.org/wiki/Universal_Declaration_of_Human_Rights). The Declaration arose out of the experience of the Second World War, and represents the first global expression of rights to which all human beings are respectfully entitled. It consists of 30 articles that have been elaborated in subsequent international treaties, regional human rights instruments, national constitutions and laws.

The International Bill of Human Rights consists of the Universal Declaration of Human Rights, the International Covenant on Economics and Social and Cultural Rights, as well the International Covenant on Civil and Political Rights and its two Optional Protocols. In 1966, the UN General Assembly adopted the two detailed Covenants, which complete the International Bill of Human Rights. In 1976, after the Covenant had been ratified by a sufficient number of individual member states, the Bill took on the force of international law.

The morals and values of human rights may be traced back through history of religious beliefs and cultures around the world. Early European philosophers developed theories of natural law that eventually influenced the adoption of documents such as the Bill of Rights (1689) in England, the Bill of Rights (1791) in the USA and the Declaration of the Rights of Man and of the Citizen (1789) in France.

During the Second World War the Allies adopted the Four Freedoms, namely, freedom of speech, freedom of assembly, freedom from fear and freedom from want, as their basic war aims. The United Nations Charter reiterated its faith in fundamental human rights, as well as the dignity and worth of human beings. The UN committed all of its member states to promote universal respect for, and observance of, human rights and fundamental freedoms for all, without distinction as to race, sex, language or religion.

The experience of the Second World War convinced the peoples of the world that the UN Charter did not sufficiently define the rights it advanced. A universal declaration that specified the rights of individuals was necessary to give effect to the Charter's provisions of basic human rights.

The document starts with a preamble consisting of seven paragraphs, followed by the proclamation of the Declaration. As a common standard of achievement for all peoples, it calls on all individuals and organs of society, through teaching and education, to promote respect for those rights and freedoms and to secure their universal and effective recognition and observance through progressive national and international measures.

The following is a reproduction of the 30 articles of the Declaration that set out the specific human rights that are recognised. The contents of the Declaration are given in abbreviated form, but all rights and freedoms are included:

- All humans are born free and equal in dignity and rights. They are endowed with reason and conscience and should act towards one another in the spirit and brotherhood.
- Everyone is entitled to all rights and freedoms set forth in the Declaration, without any distinction such as race, colour, sex, language, religion, political or other opinion, national or social origin, property, birth or other status. Also, no distinction may be made on the basis of political, jurisdictional or international status of the country or territory to which a person belongs, whether it is independent, trust, non-governing or under any other limitation or sovereignty.
- Everyone has a right of life, liberty and security of person.
- No one may be held in slavery or servitude. Slavery and the slave trade are prohibited in all their forms.
- No one may be subjected to torture or to cruel, inhuman or degrading treatment or punishment.
- Everyone has the right to recognition everywhere as a person before the law.
- All are equal before the law and are entitled without any discrimination to equal protection of the law. All are entitled to equal protection against any discrimination in violation of the Declaration and against any incitement to such discrimination.
- Everybody has a right to effective remedy by the competent national tribunals for acts violating their fundamental rights granted to them by the constitution or by law.
- No one may be subjected to arbitrary arrest, detention or exile.
- Everybody is entitled, fully equal, to a fair and public hearing by an independent and impartial tribunal in the determination of their rights and obligations and in any criminal charge against them.
- Everybody charged with a penal offence have the right to be presumed innocent until proved guilty according to law in a public trial at which they have had all the guarantees necessary for their defence.
- Also, nobody may be held guilty of any penal offence on account of any act or omission that did not constitute a penal offence, under national or international law, at the time when it was committed, and a heavier penalty may not be imposed than the one that was applicable at the time the penal offence was committed.
- Nobody may be subjected to arbitrary interference in their privacy,

family, home or correspondence and also not to attacks on their honour or reputation. Everybody has the right to protection by the law against such interference or attacks.

- Everybody has the right to freedom of movement and residence within the borders of each state, and everybody has the right to leave any country, including their own, and to return to their country.
- Everybody has the right to seek and enjoy in any other country asylum from persecution. However, that right may not be invoked in cases of prosecution genuinely arising from non-political crimes or from acts contrary to the purposes and principles of the United Nations.
- Everybody has the right to a nationality and nobody may be deprived of their nationality nor denied the right to change their nationality.
- Men and women of full age, without any limitation due to race, nationality or religion, have the right to marry and found a family, and they are entitled to equal rights as to marriage, during marriage and at its conclusion. However, marriage shall be entered into only with the full consent of the intending spouses. Further, the family is the natural and fundamental group unit of society and is entitled to protection by society and the state.
- Everyone has the right to own property alone as well as in association with others, and nobody may arbitrarily be deprived of their property.
- Everybody has the right to freedom of thought, conscience and religion. This right includes the right to change their religion of belief and freedom, either alone or in community with others and in public or private, to manifest their religion or belief in teaching, practice, worship and observance.
- Everyone has the right to freedom of expression. This right includes freedom to hold opinions without interference and to seek, receive and impart information and ideas through any media and regardless of frontiers.
- Everyone has the right to freedom of peaceful assembly and association, and no one may be compelled to belong to an association.
- Everybody has the right to take part in the government of their country, directly or through freely chosen representatives. Further, everyone has the right to equal access to public service in their country.
- The will of the people must be the basis of the authority of government, and this must be expressed in periodic and genuine elections that have

to be universal and equal suffrage and must be held by secret vote or by equivalent free voting procedures.

- Everybody, as members of society, have the right to social security and are entitled to realisation, through national effort and international cooperation and in accordance with the organisation and resources of each state, of the economic, social and cultural rights indispensable for their dignity and the free development of their personalities.
- Everybody has the right to work, to free choice of employment, to just and favourable conditions of work and to protection against unemployment, and everybody, without discrimination, has the right to equal pay for equal work.
- Everybody who works has the right to a just and favourable remuneration, ensuring for themselves and their families an existence worthy of human dignity, and supplemented, if necessary, by other means of social protection.
- Everybody has the right to form and join trade unions for the protection of their interests.
- Everyone has the right to rest and leisure, including reasonable limitation of working hours and periodic holidays and pay.
- Everybody has the right to a standard of living adequate for the health and wellbeing of themselves and of their families, including food, clothing and medical care and necessary social service, and the right to security in the event of unemployment, sickness, disability, widowhood, old age and other lack of livelihood in circumstances beyond their control.
- Motherhood and childhood are entitled to special care and assistance. All children, whether born in or out of wedlock, must enjoy the same social protection.
- Everyone has the right to education. Education must be free, at least in the elementary and fundamental stages. Elementary education must be compulsory. Technical and professional education must be made generally available and higher education must be equally accessible to all on the basis of merit.
- Education must be directed to the full development of the human personality and to the strengthening of respect for human rights and fundamental freedoms. It must promote understanding, tolerance, and friendship among all nations, racial or religious groups and must

further the activities of the United Nations for the maintenance of peace.

- Parents have a prior right to choose the kind of education that may be given to their children.
- Everyone has the right to participate freely in the cultural life of the community, to enjoy the arts and to share in scientific advancement and its benefits.
- Everybody has the right to the protection of the moral and material interests resulting from any scientific, literary or artistic production of which they are the authors.
- Everyone is entitled to a social and international order in which the rights and freedoms set forth in the Declaration may be fully realised.
- Everybody has duties to the community in which alone the free and full development of their personalities is possible.
- In the exercise of their rights and freedoms, everybody may be subject only to such limitations as are determined by law solely for the purpose of securing due recognition and respect for the rights and freedoms of others and of meeting the just requirements of morality, public order and the general welfare in a democratic society.
- These rights and freedoms may in no case be exercised contrary to the purpose and principles of the United Nations.
- Nothing in the Declaration may be interpreted as implying for any state, group or person any right to engage in any activity or to perform any act aimed at the destruction of any of the rights and freedoms set out in it.

5.5 South African Constitution

The South African Constitution, 1996, which commenced on 4 February 1997, is a comprehensive document covering what the founding body regarded as necessary to move the country into an era of true democracy. It starts with a number of founding provisions and a comprehensive bill of rights. The further provisions of the Constitution cover the spheres of government and their functional areas, judicial bodies, institutions supporting constitutional democracy, public administration, security services, traditional leaders and public finance. It ends with general provisions covering such things as international law, the national flag, oaths and solemn affirmations, and election procedures. What is of importance for the purposes of this book is the system of democratic values established by the Constitution.

5.5.1 Founding provisions

The founding provisions establish, for the first time, that there is a common South African citizenship. All citizens are equally entitled to the rights, privileges and benefits of citizenship. They are also equally subject to the duties and responsibilities of citizenship. Provision is made for the acquisition, loss and restoration of citizenship.

Provision is made for eleven official languages and that all official languages must enjoy parity of esteem and be treated equitably. A Pan South African Language Board (PANSALB) is created to bring about conditions for the development and use of all official languages, as well as other indigenous languages and sign language. The Board also has to promote respect for languages commonly used by certain communities, as well as certain languages used for religious purposes.

5.5.2 South African Bill of Rights

Section 7(1) of the Constitution states: 'The Bill of Rights is a cornerstone of democracy in South Africa. It enshrines the rights of all people in our country and affirms the democratic values of human dignity, equality and freedom.' However, section 7(3) cautions that the rights defined in the Bill are subject to limitations contained in section 36 and elsewhere in the Bill. Section 36(1) states that they may be limited, but only in terms of law of general application, provided that the limitation is reasonable and justifiable in an open and democratic society, based on human dignity, equality and freedom and taking into account all relevant factors, some of which are stipulated in that subsection. Except for this limitation and other provisions of the Constitution, no law may limit any rights entrenched in the Bill.

Anybody referred to in the Bill has the right to approach a competent court to claim that a right in the Bill of Rights has been contravened or that a contravention is immanent, and the court may extend legal aid, including a declaration of rights.

The Bill of Rights further develops what has been entrenched in the founding provisions:

- Everyone is equal before the law.
- Everyone has the right to have their dignity respected and protected.

- Everyone has the right to life.
- Everyone has the right to freedom and security of the person.
- No one may be subjected to slavery, servitude or forced labour.
- Everyone has the right to privacy.
- Everyone has the right to freedom of conscience, religion, thought, belief and opinion.
- Everyone has the right to freedom of expression.
- Everyone has the right, peacefully and unarmed, to assemble, demonstrate, picket and present petitions.
- Everyone has the right to freedom of association.
- Every citizen is free to make political choices, including forming a political party, participating in the activities of or recruiting members for a political party, and campaigning for a political party or cause.
- Every citizen has the right to free, fair and regular elections; to cast secret votes in elections; and to stand and hold public office.
- No citizen may be deprived of citizenship.
- Everyone has the right to freedom of movement, including to move freely in South Africa, to leave the country, and the right to a passport.
- Everyone has the right to fair labour practices.
- Everyone has the right to an environment that is not harmful, to have the environment protected for the benefit of present and future generations.
- No one may be deprived of property, except in terms of law of general application.
- Everyone has the right to have access to adequate housing.
- Everyone has the right to health care services, sufficient food and water, and social security.
- The best interests of children are of the utmost importance. Every child (anybody under 18 years of age) has the right to a name and a nationality from birth, to family or parental care or to appropriate alternative care when the child is taken from the family environment. Children also have the right to basic food, shelter, basic health care and social services, and are protected against such things as maltreatment, humiliation, detainment and abuse of any kind. Furthermore, children may not be detained except under exceptional circumstances and then only for as short a period as possible.
- Everybody has the right to basic education (including basic education for adults) and to further education that the government has to

reasonably supply on an ever-increasing basis.

- Everyone has the right, in compliance with the Bill of Rights, to use the language of their choice and to participate in their choice of cultural life.
- Nobody may be denied the right to participate in the activities of their cultural, religious, or language communities, together with other members of those communities, provided that this is consistent with the provisions of the Bill of Rights.
- Everyone has the right of access to any public information and that which is held by anyone else and which is necessary in pursuit of any rights.
- Everyone has the right to legal, reasonable and procedurally fair administrative action, and when anybody's rights have been detrimentally affected by administrative action, they have the right to reasons being given in writing.
- Everyone has the right that a dispute that could be settled by law may be settled in a fair public hearing before a court or, where appropriate, another independent and unbiased tribunal or forum.
- Anybody arrested because of an alleged transgression has many rights, including to remain silent, to be informed of their rights, to be charged at their first court appearance, not to be held longer than 48 hours, and to be set free under reasonable terms should this be in the interests of justice. Furthermore, all prisoners have the right to be informed, in the language of their choice, of the reason for their captivity, to be represented by legal counsel and to receive specified visitors. Finally, any accused person has the right to a fair trial, including to be informed of the charge and to be able to plead, to have sufficient time and facilities to prepare a defence and to have the trial concluded within a reasonable period of time.
- The rights of the Bill may only be restricted in terms of a generally valid legal restriction to the extent to which the restriction is fair and justified in an open democratic society, based on human dignity, equity and freedom, with due regard to all relevant factors, including the nature of law, the importance of the purpose of the restriction, the nature and extent of the restriction, the relationship between the restriction, and in a less restrictive way to achieve the purpose.
- A state of emergency may be declared only in terms of an Act of Parliament, and only under certain conditions, and it may be subjected to a ruling by a court of law.

In short, certain rights are inviolable in full or provisionally:

- Equity
- Human dignity
- Life
- Freedom and personal security
- Slavery, servitude and forced labour
- Those of children
- Those of arrested, detained and accused persons.

In interpreting the Bill of Rights, a court, tribunal or forum must promote the values fundamental to and in an open and democratic society, based on human dignity, equity and freedom, must take cognisance of international law and may take into account external law. Also, when interpreting any statues and in developing common law, each court, tribunal or forum should promote the spirit, extent and objectives of the Bill of Rights. Lastly, the Bill of Rights does not refute the existence of other rights and freedoms recognised or granted by common law or legislation, to the extent that those rights and freedoms are compatible with the Bill.

5.5.3 Cooperative government

The government of South Africa consists of national, provincial and local spheres of government that are distinct, mutually dependent and interdependent. All spheres of government have to uphold the principles contained in the Constitution and must execute their activities within the limits imposed by the Constitution.

All spheres of government and all organs of state within each sphere must:

- maintain peace, national unity and the indivisibility of the country;
- ensure the welfare of the country's people;
- provide effective, transparent, accountable and coherent government for the country as a whole;
- be loyal to the country's Constitution and its people;
- respect the constitutional status, institutions, authority and functions of the other spheres;
- not take upon themselves any authority or functions, except those committed to them by the Constitution;
- not execute their authority and deliver their functions in a way that will

encroach upon the geographical, functional or institutional integrity in another sphere;
- in mutual reliance and trust cooperate with each other in a friendly, supportive, information sharing, coordinated, agreed procedural way, and by avoiding legal action against each other.

5.5.4 Governmental structure

The government of South Africa consists of a central government (parliament), provincial councils and local governments.

The central government consists of Parliament (the National Assembly and the National Council of Provinces), the civil service (which it shares with the various provinces), central and provincial government enterprises and a variety of parastatals. The three distinct fields of operation of the central government and provincial governments are the legislative, executive and judicial authorities.

Legislative authority

In terms of the Constitution, the National Assembly and the National Council of Provinces participate in the legislative process. This means that it may, inter alia, amend the Constitution and any area provided for in the Constitution, but excluding areas in which provinces have exclusive legislative competence, such as those related to abattoirs and provincial cultural matters. It may also assign some of its legislative authority to other spheres of government. Therefore, the two houses of Parliament are only governed by the Constitution, and it has to act in terms of and within the limits of the Constitution.

The members of the National Assembly are elected by popular vote and on a proportional basis at intervals of five years in national elections. The Assembly makes legislative decisions as a whole, but much of its operations are underpinned by the work done by select and joint committees appointed from among its membership.

The National Council of Provinces is composed of a single delegation from each province consisting of ten members. Each delegation consists of members nominated by their respective legislatures and is usually composed of representatives of political parties within each of those legislatures.

Each provincial legislature is also elected by popular vote on a proportional basis and has legislative authority in terms of the Constitution, which includes areas such as health, education and security services. Provincial councils have limited sources of revenue and are dependent on grants and subsidies from the national legislature.

In the local sphere, there are a variety of local governments, from metropolitan councils to town and district councils. All of these councils are elected by popular vote on both a proportional and a ward basis. This means that local councils consist, on the one hand, of a number of representatives elected in terms of the percentage of votes cast for their parties at an election relative to the number of seats available. On the other hand, individual candidates are elected in each of the wards that constitute the area of jurisdiction of each council. Therefore, elections for members of local councils do not coincide with elections for the national and provincial legislatures.

Local councils have wide areas of legislative authority in terms of the Constitution and specific national legislation. They also have unique sources of revenue, such as property tax and specific other rates and taxes

In legislation, the laws and by-laws of provincial and local legislators may not be in conflict with those of the central government. The central government, in turn, may not legislate in conflict with the Constitution.

Executive authority

Each sphere of government has its own executive. In the central government sphere, the national Cabinet is the executive authority. The Cabinet consists of the President, Deputy President(s) and the other Ministers of State appointed by the President in portfolios on which the Cabinet decides. The Cabinet is the body that formulates national public policy.

Provincial governments have their own executive authorities, consisting of the premier of each province and provincial members of executive councils (MECs, popularly also known as ministers) appointed to various portfolios.

Various executive authorities are constituted in the local sphere of government. Some local governments have appointed chief executives, while others have chairpersons elected from local legislatures, who appoint elected members to various local portfolios.

Obviously, there are overlapping executive areas that could lead to clashes between the central executive, the provincial executives and the local executives. Most of these aspects are dealt with by specific constitutional provisions and other legislation on cooperative government.

Judicial authority

Various courts operate in all spheres. The highest courts in South Africa are the Constitutional Court and the Supreme Court of Appeal. All but two provinces have a high court (and those two are in the process of being established). In the local sphere, there are magistrate courts in magisterial districts to serve local needs. There are also various specialised courts of appeal, as well as other courts in wide-ranging areas such as water affairs.

Civil service

There are various central government departments specialising in matters ranging from foreign affairs to safety and security and defence, each with its own managerial structure under direct control of a minister of state and, therefore, directly accountable to Parliament. The provinces also have their various departments, with their managerial structures under direct control of a provincial minister. The provincial functionaries are therefore directly accountable to their provincial executives, and indirectly accountable to Parliament. The departments of both the central government and the provincial governments form the civil service.

Local administrations

Each local government has its own functional departments under direct control of an elected local member appointed to oversee each department. These departments have their own functional structures and are officially directly accountable to their local executive and indirectly accountable to the relevant provincial government and to the central government.

Government enterprises and parastatals

In areas where governments (in all spheres) need specialised goods and service delivery, where the government is unwilling to leave, wholly or partially, such functions to private enterprise, and where the private sector is either unable or unwilling to deliver those goods and services, the governments themselves have to establish such enterprises. These enterprises are partly financed from government grants and subsidies and payment by the public for goods and services delivered. Therefore, they are partly government-controlled and partly market-oriented.

5.5.5 Core public sector business

The core business of a government is the delivery of public goods and services within the areas of safety and security (domestic and foreign), economic stability and judicial control. For these purposes, certain government departments are created. These departments are staffed by personnel who are employed in terms of service conditions prescribed by the government of the day. Moreover, in order to fulfil its core functions, government operates at various levels or in various spheres. Depending on a specific constitution and the ideology of the government of the day, a government may concentrate merely on its core business, at the one extreme, or take total control of a country in all respects, at the other. Many variations between these extremes are possible. In the most extreme cases, a country can exist as a political entity without a government for a period of time.

5.5.6 Public policy

A government governs in execution of, and in terms of, public policy, based on its ideology, mostly formulated and executed in terms of a constitution. A government may suspend a constitution temporarily or permanently or take total control in terms of a token constitution.

In a democracy, a government in theory governs in terms of the authority accorded to it by a country's citizens, who have the power to dismiss that government. The authority should be accorded on the strength of a political party's proposed policies, but party loyalties play a major role. In theory, a government delivers goods and services to all of a country's citizens, within and outside of a country's boundaries.

Public policy, briefly stated, is what governments decide to do or not to do. Some of the characteristics of public policy are as follows:

- It arises from a process over time.
- It is not decision-making or administration.
- It involves behaviour as well as intentions, and inaction as well as action.
- It has outcomes that may or may not have been foreseen.
- It is a purposive course of action (although purpose may be defined retrospectively).
- It involves intra- and inter-organisational relationships, and a key, but not exclusive, role for public institutions.
- it is subjectively defined.

As stated, public policy arises from a process. This process consists of a number of stages, and each of these stages form part of a chain of the system of public values, because in practice public policy is made by political parties that contest elections. In the election campaigns of those parties, the voters are requested to vote for the party whose policies are most acceptable to them. The various stages of public policy-making are outlined below

Policy formulation

- *Deciding to decide* (issue search or agenda-setting). The identification of problems or opportunities that suggest the need for action. Some problems and opportunities are unforeseeable, but others may be identified at early stages
- *Deciding how to decide* (or issue filtration). It has to be decided how the decision has to be made. Should the issue be left to normal political and administrative processes, or should it be selected for more fundamental and objective analysis?
- *Issue definition.* Once a problem or a policy issue has been identified, it usually requires some further definition
- *Forecasting.* It is necessary to forecast how a situation will develop. It is useful to speculate about alternative possible futures, given different assumptions about the development of both problems and policies.
- *Setting objectives and priorities.* The questions to be answered are, what is the government trying to achieve, and how will it know when it has achieved it?
- *Options analysis.* Options have to be compared and appraised through advocacy or analyses such as cost-effectiveness studies, cost–benefit analysis or PAR (programme analysis and review).

For example, as far as the public value of transparency is concerned, when identifying and prioritising issues and investigating methods of addressing them, a political party that is serious in forming a government should consult the public as widely as possible.

Policy implementation and execution

When a political party has won an election, its policy remains a party-political one. Before becoming public policy, it should be adopted and priorities and options agreed to by the appropriate legislator. This often results in legislation being adopted by that legislator. When a preferred option has emerged, it is necessary to formulate and communicate the resulting policy and to engage in a more detailed design of associated programmes. Problems should be seen in advance, and procedures should be designed into the programmes. Therefore, all the principles of democratic government should come into play.

Policy monitoring and control

Once a policy and its constituent programmes are under way, progress should be monitored and attempts made to check whether performance is living up to earlier expectations. Forms of analysis may be used; where they demonstrate that programmes are not proceeding according to plan, remedial action may be necessary.

It is internationally accepted that South Africa has one of the finest constitutions in the world and that legislation supporting it is satisfactory. The generally agreed problem is that the stage of monitoring and control is inadequate and that the public, in many cases, are not receiving the public goods and services envisaged by government. In addition to the steps taken by government for the Department of the Presidency to take an overall monitoring responsibility over government departments, the Constitution, under Chapter 8, makes provision for a number of public institutions to strengthen constitutional democracy in the country.

Policy evaluation and review

At certain points (either predetermined or not), more fundamental reviews may be made of policy.

Policy maintenance, succession and termination

It is often difficult to replace or terminate a policy, even if an explicit decision has been made to do so. The chances of success are enhanced if the possibility of replacement or termination at some future date was designed into the initial policy.

5.6 Public resources

All public resources have to be managed in a specific manner. This is so because they are public resources that are procured and managed by government in terms of specific legislation, regulations, rules and policies, and to the benefit of a specific community or society. Mainly human, capital/financial, information and natural environmental resources are at stake.

5.6.1 Goods and service delivery to all citizens

In terms of a March 2004 judgment by the High Court, the South African government is required to extend poverty allowances, not only to South African citizens, but also to non-citizens who have been accorded permanent residence. Therefore, public goods and services are made available on a wide scale even to non-citizens, as they already enjoy the basic rights accorded to them by the Constitution.

Goods and services

In terms of the country's Constitution, court rulings and the public policies prevalent since the 2009 general elections, goods and services are delivered as follows:

- **All citizens:** In a democratic country like South Africa, this means everyone from birth to demise and whether they are within the country or outside its borders. In most cases this extends to non-citizens, but generally they are not entitled to certain rights and privileges, such as voting in elections, As far as foreign citizens are concerned, the public policy may stringently be applied and not allow them to work within the country on any account or to allow it under certain conditions, or the policy may be to relax such control measures for a time. In South Africa's case, the present phase of transition plays an important role.
- **Delivery:** At present, the government's policies on how public goods and services are to be delivered are contained in the *Batho Pele* White Paper. This covers eight principles and how to put them into practice.
- **Types of goods and services:** At present, the government is involved in all sectors of the country's socio-economic life. This is because of the challenges facing it – mainly poverty, unemployment, growth, crime, education and health.

5.7 The public budget

The one area of public sector financial management that is indeed unique is the public budget in all spheres of government. It is unique in its formulation, execution and control processes.

5.7.1 Introduction

The society to which South African society aspires – compassionate, democratic, and egalitarian – will not come about by belief alone, but it is a society the country's citizens seek to create. They create it in their communities when someone who has never had running water opens a tap, or when a family turns on an electric light for the first time. In their region, when they join in a compact with others, they seek to negotiate a new partnership for the sustainable development of the continent. They also seek it in an international order committed to the eradication of poverty.

The two decades of globalisation, leading up to 2009, were characterised by unbridled optimism, by the longest period of growth in the USA, the prospects of economic power embodied in the coming of age of the European Union (EU), and the mirage of unimpeded expansion in Asia and Latin America. With the global economic meltdown of 2008–2009, this came to a standstill as far as Africa is concerned.

The wave of globalisation had three characteristics:

- A group of developing countries became players in global markets.
- International migration and capital movements increased, reshaping trading patterns and ownership structures.
- For some developing countries, globalisation led to increased marginalisation.

Unprecedented prosperity and wealth in developed nations have created opportunities for growth and trade for other countries. However, these benefits have not been distributed equally. The bulk of capital flows remain between the rich countries. A naive definition of success has blunted the world's commitment to address poverty. It has ignored local realities, cultures and needs and sought simplistic answers to complex problems.

The poor are remarkably peace-loving. It is the poorest of the poor who are the victims of violence and terrorism. The reason South Africa needs to combat poverty is because it deprives individuals of their full potential. It robs children of their childhood, condemns adults to illiteracy, deprives people of access to simple necessities, condemns many millions to disease, wears down the human spirit and robs people of their dignity. The country has to fight poverty because until it has been overcome, citizens cannot lay claim to South Africa being a compassionate society. A society that recognises and respects the richness of its different cultures and languages and the humanity of all of the world's peoples, recognises that the life of a Third World child is a precious as that of a First World child, and accepts that poverty anywhere lessens the humanity of every citizen of the globe. This is a society that actively seeks human solidarity. Solidarity is not discovered by reflection but created by increasing people's sensitivity to the details of the pain and humiliation of other, unfamiliar people.

From the global economic perspective, the challenge faced by South Africa is to ensure that the gains that have been made through globalisation can be extended to eliminate poverty and improve *equity* in the poorest parts of the world.

5.7.2 South African public budget

The budget gives priority to reducing poverty and vulnerability. Therefore, it increases spending on social grants, municipal infrastructure and housing, improved police and justice services and critical administrative services to citizens. It also supports an enhanced programme to address the impact of HIV/AIDS, and gives continued emphasis to infrastructural development to encourage development and job creation in support of urban and rural development.

The budget further supports the government's budget responsibilities by strengthening the fight against crime. It also steps up assistance to communities to improve access to affordable basic services, and gives tax relief to all. South Africa appropriates a considerable part of its national budget to education.

The government obviously recognises the importance of taking charge of the country's destiny and of finding solutions that are appropriate for its needs and circumstances. The response has been to seek a partnership with the global economy and, in particular, the wealthy nations, and multilateral institutions, such as the United Nations (UN), Organisation for Economic Cooperation and Development (OECD), the Indian Ocean Rim – Association for Regional Cooperation (IOR – ARC), and the International Monetary Fund (IMF). This is a partnership based on trust, respect and a commitment to succeed, designed to improve the quality of the lives of all the people of Africa (in particular the poor) and to contribute positively to global growth and prosperity. All South Africans have a shared responsibility to ensure that this partnership takes root and grows. The intention is to place on the agenda of the global discourse the values and principles that have guided our young democracy.

Economic outlook

There is a need to address broader social policy concerns alongside growth as an economic goal. Public action in areas such as education, health, social development, security, land reform and housing are critical to a development strategy that places at its core the need to eradicate poverty and create a better life for all citizens. The budget makes five key interventions in support of development and the war against poverty:

- It is strongly oriented towards growth.
- It provides for an intensification of spending to alleviate poverty, including increases in old-age pensions and child support grants and an enhanced response to HIV/AIDS.
- There is increased investment in infrastructure, especially in support of urban renewal and rural development.
- It strengthens the fight against crime, e.g. by making available the resources to employ additional police personnel.
- It provides tax cuts for individuals, tax incentives for investment and a more generous tax regime for small businesses.

The South African economy is not immune to the international developments that have temporarily unsettled growth and inflation trends. However, growth of the country's economy has been underpinned by extensive structural reforms designed to ensure a more dynamic and resilient economy.

5.7.3 Government goals and objectives

A government exists for various reasons, mostly political. However, a government's existence is also due to financial factors. The extent of its involvement in the financial system of a country to a large extent determines the size and power of a government. If it controls all of a country's financial and other resources, then it will have a large bureaucracy and total power. This is true of totalitarian regimes. If, on the other hand, government controls only those financial resources essential to the survival of the country, it will have a small bureaucracy and authority conferred upon it by an electorate. The following factors, to a greater or lesser extent, determine the size and extent of the public financial sector:

- measures to secure appropriate market factors;
- regulation where decreasing costs cause competitive inefficiency;
- regulations to control contractual arrangements and exchanges

regarding market operations;
- direct involvement in cases of market failure;
- adjustments in income distribution due to societal values;
- public sector involvement may be necessary to generate high employment, price-level stability and/or a socially desirable economic growth;
- subsidising necessary private goods where the market is unable to do so.

Public norms and values determine the basic economic policy and policy objectives adopted by a government. The public policy objectives that may be determined are outlined below.

Policy objectives

As a government has many political, social, economic and other objectives, it is necessary for it to formulate and execute the appropriate policies in order to realise those objectives. In a financial sense, a government has the following objectives:

- **The allocation function:** This is a process of securing the efficient provision of social goods. Certain goods, called 'social' to distinguish them from 'private' goods, cannot be provided through transactions between consumers and producers, that is, the market system. In a market economy, this happens when the market functions inefficiently or fails. The difficulty a government has lies in deciding the type and quality of social goods. For example, at what level and to what extent should a government provide security services to companies and firms, and when may they decide to let them provide their own security? Another difficulty is that all goods are not neatly divided into social and private goods. This means that a government may, in certain circumstances, interfere with consumer preferences without meaning to do so. It is important to note that social goods are provided publicly. They are financed through the public budget and made available free of direct charge. How they are produced does not matter.
- **The distribution function:** Distributing social goods is perhaps the most important and controversial point in public policy, because social goods play a key role in determining taxation and transfer policies. In order to be socially equitable, a government, especially one in a developing country, should regard distribution and redistribution as priorities.

- **The stabilisation function:** A government's fiscal policy has to be designed to maintain and achieve the goals of high employment, a reasonable degree of price level stability, soundness in foreign financial matters, and an acceptable rate of economic growth. Without these, the economy will be subject to fluctuations and suffer periods of high unemployment and/or inflation. Public policy must be designed to deal with these contingencies, but it may, if poorly conducted, be a destabiliser itself.

Financial planning

Planning and budgeting are the most prevalent of all the public management processes related to finance. They form the core of financial management and are closely associated with both policy-making and control. Planning and budgeting may be seen as a sequential process divisible into the following overlapping stages:

- **Long-term financial planning:** A long-term financial plan has to be comprehensive, and various procedures may be used to ensure extensive plans. It should be constructed in combination with statutory structure plans, taking into account public policies and legislation. Formal plans also take into account the ever-changing environment.
- **Strategic planning:** Strategic public financial planning could be successfully adapted to the situation and the specific needs of public financial context. Strategic planning is a continuous process, divisible into the three phases of strategy formulation, strategy implementation and strategy evaluation.
- **Intermediate planning:** The intermediate stage typically covers a period of about five years. The characteristics of an intermediate plan include financial considerations, greater precision and the translation of statements of broad aim into concrete action. It records decisions relating to different ways of achieving goals and objectives, puts ongoing and projected activities into perspective, and provides data for revising long-term plans. It is important to note that it is the starting point of the annual budget. In many systems the first year of an intermediate plan is expanded to form the annual budget.
- **Operational planning:** This is short-term (one-year) planning, giving effect to the longer-term strategic plan. The annual budget, comprising both capital and revenue, represents the final stage of financial

planning. From this are set departmental targets for the year, laying down the basis of accountability. The annual budget is the cornerstone of a public institution's financial arrangements.

Financial decision-making

In a representative democracy, the representatives of the voters and taxpayers decide public financial matters. In this system, the public become spectators, in contrast to a participatory democracy, where taxpayers and voters are active players. The possibility emerges that the decisions made by representatives and their bureaucracies could conflict with the wishes of those voters and taxpayers whose interests they represent. Therefore, certain links between the public and financial decision-makers are necessary.

Interest groups, including social establishments, sports bodies, religious institutions and community forums, form the link between voters and the bureaucracy. Individuals are hardly able to exert influence on the public decision-making process and therefore need the support of an interest group that can lobby for them. From the point of view of interest groups, they may regard the financial decision-making process as a method by which individuals within the group can articulate their interests to the public decision-makers. In general, interest groups can be divided into those who continually demand less taxes and government involvement and those who demand ever-better social goods and services and more government involvement.

One objection raised against interest groups is that individuals with a similar interest do not always succeed in forming true interest groups, or that the interests of different groups are not always represented with the same effectiveness, as in confederations of labour unions. Therefore, it remains the task of financial decision-makers to strike a balance between the demands, claims, requests and representations of the different interest groups. Not only that, but they also have to educate the public that in all cases of goods and service delivery someone has to foot the bill, and the higher the demands, the more may be spent to meet them and the less can be spent on other essential goods and services.

5.7.4 **Budgeting**

From a government's perspective, the annual budget is often the principal vehicle for developing government plans and policies. Combined with the planning process, the budget states specific amounts of money relative to government activities, and these decisions reflect the government's plans and policies more accurately than most planning documents. The budget can be defined as follows (Schwella *et al*, 1996:127):

> *A budget is a plan for achieving goals and objectives within a definite time limit, containing estimates of resources required, together with estimates of sources available, usually compared with one or more past periods and showing future requirements.*

If a public body had all the money it wanted, it probably would not have to write budgets. However, there is never enough money to do all that needs to be done. Money is a scarce resource, and, as a result, some things have to be forgone in favour of other things that have to be done. This is where budgets come in. By listing clearly and systematically all the things on which to expend money, this scarce resource can be spent sensibly (Huddleston, 1992:145–146). Guarding against financial imprudence is not the only reason to budget, however. A second reason a government budgets is to ensure that money is spent only in accordance with specified public objectives. Budgets provide the means for citizens and public officials to control or account for the expenditure of public funds. Instead of merely transferring funds from the treasury at the beginning of each fiscal year, a budget is drawn up that specifies in detail what should be purchased, and how much should be spent on these items and the delivery of specified public goods and services. It also requires that account be given of such expenditure.

Finally, budgets assist in making decisions. By classifying alternative expenditures in ways that allow systematic comparison, public officials can make informed choices about which investments of public funds promise the best return. For example, it is possible to devise budget systems that help officials weigh the relative merits of two training schemes or decide whether certain security activities serve a community better than others.

The thousands of different specific approaches used by various governments are merely variations on a few themes. There are four basic budget systems, namely, line-item budgeting, performance budgeting, programme budgeting and zero-base budgeting. These systems represent a historical progression in ideas about budgeting. However, later ideas have not actually replaced earlier ideas. New techniques or formats have been developed as demands on budget systems have changed. In general, the line of progression has been from less complex to more complex, as budgeting systems have been required to undertake more and more tasks.

PRINCIPLES, VALUES AND NORMS PRESENTED IN THIS CHAPTER

Legal precedent
Ultra vires
Universal and South African human rights
Equity
Human dignity
Life
Freedom and personal security
Slavery, servitude and forced labour
Children's rights
Detainee's rights
Provisions of good governance
Power and authority of governments in all spheres
Core public sector business is the delivery of public goods and services
Ethics of public policy-making
Public goods and service delivery to all citizens
Unique public budget
Democratic control of public finances
Public norms and values control basic public economic policy

Having studied this chapter, how would you now answer the question posed at the beginning?
Write a comparative essay on the United Nations Universal Declaration of Human Rights and the South African Bill of Rights.

Chapter 6

Constitutional and constitutionally based policy and legislation

IN THIS CHAPTER

After reading this chapter, you should be able to:

- explain the role of institutions such as the Public Protector, the Human Rights Commission, the Commission for the Promotion and Protection of the Rights of Cultural, Religious and Language Communities and the Commission for Gender Equality;
- discuss the importance of the office of the Auditor-General;
- explain the function of the Electoral Commission
- explain the role of the Independent Broadcasting Regulatory Authority;
- evaluate the principles and policy of *Batho Pele*;
- explain the processes of benchmarking.

Before studying this chapter, see if you can answer the following question:
Are you able to define the term *Batho Pele*?

6.1 Introduction

The South African Constitution contains provisions to ensure that its requirements are honoured and that the constitutional rights of citizens are honoured. In addition, legislation has been promulgated to further protect the rights of citizens and communities. This body of legislation

Ability to deliver acceptable services is not a criterion.

also established various institutions and has made a number of policies to give further effect to constitutional provisions. This chapter examines a number of these, but does not claim to be a full and final account of all legislation, institutions and policies. What is included in this chapter is a personal selection from a wide variety.

6.2 Public institutions in support of constitutional democracy

The South African Constitution, in Chapter 9, provides for a number of institutions that have to assist governments to strengthen constitutional democracy in the country. These institutions operate independently and are subject to constitutional provisions alone; have the unbiased support and protection of organs of state; may not be interfered with by any person or organ of state; and are accountable to Parliament in annual reports on their activities and execution of duties. These reports must be publicly accessible. The authority conferred upon these institutions covers the principles and values enshrined in the Constitution.

6.2.1 Public Protector

The Public Protector, regulated by national legislation and appointed for a non-recurring period of seven years, is authorised to act in all activities of state or the public service in any sphere of government alleged or presumed to be improper or harmful. However, the Public Protector may not investigate court decisions and must be accessible to all persons and communities.

6.2.2 Human Rights Commission

The Human Rights Commission must promote respect for and a culture of human rights, promote the protection, development and realisation of human rights and monitor and determine its prevalent state in the country.

The commission, as regulated by national legislation, also has the authority necessary to perform its functions, which include:

- to investigate and report on the maintenance of human rights;
- to take steps in order to ensure appropriate recovery where human rights have been violated;
- to initiate research;
- to educate.

Furthermore, the commission must annually require relevant organs of state to supply information about the measures taken by them in realisation of the rights in the Bill of Rights regarding housing, health care, food, water, welfare security, education and the environment.

6.2.3 Commission for the Promotion and Protection of the Rights of Cultural, Religious and Language Communities

The main objectives of the commission are as follows:

- promote respect regarding the rights of cultural, religious and language communities;
- promote and develop peace, friendship, compassion, tolerance and national unity among cultural, religious and language communities on the basis of equity, non-discrimination and free association;
- recommend the founding or acknowledgement, in terms of national legislation, of cultural or other councils for communities.

The commission is authorised to investigate, research, educate, gather support, advise and report, as regulated by national legislation, on what is necessary to achieve its main objectives, including matters regarding the rights of cultural, religious and language groups.

In addition, the commission has the authority and function prescribed by national legislation.

6.2.4 Commission for Gender Equality

The commission must promote respect for and the development of protection and realisation of gender equality. Furthermore, the commission has the necessary authority, as regulated by national legislation, to execute its functions, including the authority to monitor, investigate, research, educate and gather support on matters relating to gender equality.

6.2.5 Auditor-General

The Auditor-General, appointed for a fixed, non-repeatable period of between five and ten years, must audit and report on the accounts, financial statements and financial management of all national and provincial government departments and administrations, as well as all municipalities and any other institution or accounting organisation that has to be audited by the Auditor-General in terms of national or provincial legislation. Furthermore, and in addition to any legislation, the Auditor-General may audit and report on the accounts, financial statements and financial management of any institution financed from the national or a provincial revenue fund or funded by a municipality, and any institution that is authorised, in terms of any legislation, to receive funds for a public purpose.

The Auditor-General must submit audit reports to any legislator that has a direct interest in the audit, as well as to any other authority prescribed by national legislation, and all those reports must be made public. The Auditor-General also has additional authority prescribed by national legislation promulgated from time to time.

6.2.6 Electoral Commission

The Electoral Commission (often referred to by the media as the Independent Electoral Commission) must manage elections of national, provincial and municipal legislative bodies in terms of national legislation, ensure that the elections are free and fair and announce the results of those elections within a period prescribed by national legislation and as soon as is reasonably possible. In addition, the commission has the authority and functions prescribed by national legislation.

The Commission consists of at least three persons, but national legislation prescribes the number of members and their term of office.

6.2.7 Independent Broadcasting Regulatory Authority

This body was established to regulate broadcasting in the public interest and to ensure that it is fair and presents a diversity of views representative of the broad South African society.

6.3 *Batho Pele* principles

In 1997, the South African government introduced an initiative to ensure better public goods and service delivery. *Batho Pele*, from a Sesotho adage meaning 'people first', is intended to transform public service delivery to citizens, and is based on basic principles contained in the Constitution. During 2003 and following subsequent elections, the government again launched concerted efforts to reaffirm its commitment to the principles of *Batho Pele*.

The eight *Batho Pele* principles were published as a policy document called the White Paper on Transforming Public Service Delivery and made specifically applicable to all central and provincial government departments. It is emphasised that the whole process should be a continual one of improving service delivery within a short while, and then setting ever-higher goals in order to reach internationally recognised standards.

In addition to the principles, the White Paper also spelled out how those principles may be put into practice, how the implementation of the principles may be monitored and how the community may be included in programmes flowing from implementation and continual improvement.

In this chapter, the setting of standards is referred to as *benchmarking*.

6.3.1 Transforming public service delivery

The *Batho Pele* White Paper was published on 1 October 1997. It has not been published as a Bill and therefore remains a public policy document. However, the principles spelt out in the document have been incorporated in certain legislation.

Batho Pele is directly applicable to central and provincial government, but it is also highly relevant to all other areas of the public service, such as local governments and parastatals. In line with the constitutional principle of cooperative government, particularly as regards the promotion of coherent government, the White Paper expects that all sectors of public administration agree to follow the principles as set out in it.

6.3.2 Principles contained in the Constitution

At this juncture, it may be necessary to revisit the principles of public service delivery contained in the Constitution of the Republic of South Africa, 1996. The following seem to be applicable:

- A high standard of professional ethics should be promoted and maintained.
- Services should be provided impartially, fairly, equitably and without bias.
- Resources should be utilised efficiently, economically and effectively.
- Peoples' needs should be responded to.
- The public should be encouraged to participate in policy-making.
- Service delivery should be accountable, transparent and development-orientated.

The White Paper requires the public service, inter alia, to identify the following:

- a mission statement for service delivery, as well as service guarantees;
- what service delivery should be provided and to what groups;
- in line with Reconstruction and Development priorities, the principles of affordability and of redirecting service delivery to areas and groups previously under-resourced;
- service delivery standards, defined outputs and targets and performance indicators, benchmarked against comparable international standards;
- monitoring and evaluation mechanisms and structures, designed to measure progress and to introduce corrective action, where appropriate;
- plans for staffing, human resource development and organisational capacity building, tailored to service delivery needs;
- redirection of human and other resources from administrative tasks to service delivery, particularly to disadvantaged groups and areas;
- financial plans that link budgets directly to service needs and personnel plans;
- potential partnerships with the private sector, non-governmental organisations and community-based organisations that will provide more effective forms of service delivery;

- the development, particularly through training, of a culture of customer care and of approaches to service delivery that are sensitive to issues of race, gender and disability;
- outline specific short, medium and long-term goals for service delivery.

6.3.3 New managerial tools

The White Paper requires the public service to employ the following new managerial tools:

- the assignment to individual managers of responsibility for delivering specific results for a specified level of resources and for obtaining value for money in utilising these resources;
- individual responsibility for results, matched with managerial authority for decisions on how resources should be utilised;
- delegation of managerial responsibility and authority to the lowest possible level;
- transparency about results achieved and resources expended.

The White Paper states that the public service is seen as still operating within over-centralised, hierarchical and rule-bound systems inherited from the previous dispensation, which makes it difficult to hold individuals to account. The following reasons are listed:

- Decision-making is diffused.
- They are focused on inputs rather than outcomes.
- They do not encourage value for money.
- They do not reward innovation and creativity.
- They reward uniformity above efficiency and responsiveness.
- They encourage inward-looking, inflexible attitudes at odds with the vision of a public service whose highest aim is optimum service delivery.

The document agrees that it would be ideal for internal management reforms to be completed before attempting to introduce a service delivery improvement programme. However, it states that this argument ignores the fact that improved service delivery is a matter of extreme urgency for the country, and that there is no choice but to tackle both internal management and service delivery reform simultaneously. The argument further fails to recognise that the cultural and management reforms that are required are of an ongoing nature. This would be achieved more speedily and effectively by prioritising service delivery. Service delivery should not be seen as the final item of the public service transformation programme, but as an integral part of it, and a catalyst for many of the management reforms that are being sought.

The White Paper states that the concept of a customer may seem inappropriate at first glance. Customer is nevertheless a useful term in the context of improving public service delivery because it embraces certain principles that are as fundamental to public service delivery as they are to the provision of services for commercial gain. To treat citizens as customers implies the following:

- listening to their views and taking account of them when making decisions about what services should be delivered;
- treating them with consideration and respect;
- making sure that the promised level and quality of service delivery are always of the highest standard;
- responding swiftly and sympathetically when standards of service fall below the promised standard.

However, it is not only the public who should be treated as customers. National, provincial, local and parastatal departments have many internal customers, such as components and institutions for whom they provide services. The *Batho Pele* initiative applies equally to these internal customers.

Measured against the 'customer' yardstick, the document states that the South African public sector has a long way to go. In many instances, there are no clearly defined standards by which to measure the delivery of services. Individual citizens have found that complaining about delivery often has little or no effect, and can in any case be a daunting and time-consuming process. Lack of information and complex regulations are also barriers to optimum delivery. All too often, it is left to individual citizens to work out for themselves what services are available, and what they are entitled to. Too many government forms are complicated and not designed with the user in mind. Too many letters are written in a stilted, impersonal style that is off-putting to those who receive them. Finding the right person to speak to, especially one who can give friendly advice, can be trying, leaving the citizen helpless, frustrated and uncertain.

Many public servants, especially those who serve the public directly, are conscious of all this, because they have to face the public's frustrations almost every day in their work. They would often like to see improvements and often have good ideas of what could be done, but they are bound by systems and practices that they believe they are helpless to change.

6.3.4 The eight principles of *Batho Pele*

- **Consultation:** Citizens should be consulted on the quality of service delivery and, wherever possible, given a choice of services on offer.
- **Service standards:** Citizens should be advised on the level and quality of service delivery so that they are aware of what to expect.
- **Access:** All citizens should have equal access to services to which they are entitled.
- **Courtesy:** Citizens should be treated with courtesy and consideration.
- **Information:** Citizens should be given full and accurate information on the service delivery to which they are entitled.
- **Openness and transparency:** Citizens should be advised on how departments are run, how much they cost and who is in charge.
- **Redress:** If the promised standard of service delivery is not met, citizens should be offered a full explanation and a speedy and effective remedy; and when complaints are made, citizens should receive a sympathetic, positive response.
- **Value for money:** Public services should be delivered economically and efficiently in order to give citizens the best possible value for money.

6.3.5 Putting the principles into practice

The White Paper states that the paragraphs on putting the principles into practice describe what national and provincial departments as well as the wider public sector will be required to do when introducing their service delivery improvement programmes.

Consulting users of services

All departments must consult regularly and systematically on the services currently provided, as well as on the provision of new basic services to those who lack them. Whatever methods are chosen, consultation must cover the entire range of existing and potential customers. It is essential that consultation should include the views of those who have previously been denied access to public services.

The results of the consultation should be reported to the appropriate body. They should also be widely published within the organisation so that all members of staff may be aware of how their services are perceived. The results must then be taken into account when decisions are made on what services are to be provided and at what level.

Setting service standards

Departments should publish standards for the level and quality of services that they will provide, including the introduction of new services to those who have previously been denied access to them. In the case of services such as health and education, national departments, in consultation with provincial departments, may set what will serve as national baseline standards. Individual provinces may then set their own standards, provided these meet or exceed the national baseline. Provincial departments may also set additional standards for aspects not covered by national norms. Similarly, departments may set intra-departmental standards. Standards must be precise and measurable, so that users may judge for themselves whether they are receiving what was promised.

Service standards must be set at a level that is demanding and realistic. Before executing them, standards have to be approved by the appropriate body. Once approved, these must be published and displayed at the point of delivery and communicated as widely as possible to all potential users so that they know what level of services they are entitled to and complain when they do not receive it. Performance against results must be regularly measured and the results published at least once a year.

Performance against standards must be reviewed annually and, as standards are met, they should progressively be raised year by year. The standards may not be reduced once they have been set. If a standard is not met, the reasons must be explained publicly and a new target date set for when it will be achieved.

Increasing access

Departments are required to specify and set targets for progressively increasing access to their services for those who have not previously received them. Service delivery programmes should therefore specifically address the need to progressively redress the disadvantages of all barriers to access.

Ensuring courtesy

Departments must specify the standards for the way in which customers should be treated. These are to be included in their departmental Code of Conduct. The performance of personnel who deal with customers must be regularly monitored, and performance that falls below the specified standards should not be tolerated. Service delivery and customer care must be included in all future training programmes, and additional training should be given to all those who deal directly with the public, whether face-to-face or on the telephone. All managers should ensure that they receive first-hand feedback from frontline personnel, and should personally visit frontline personnel at regular intervals to see for themselves what is happening.

Providing more and better information

Departments must provide full, accurate and up-to-date information on the services they provide, and who is entitled to them. Information must be provided in a variety of media and languages to meet the differing needs of different customers. There should always be a name and contact number for obtaining further information and advice.

Increasing openness and transparency

The public should know more about the way departments are run, how well they perform, the resources they consume and who is in charge. Reports to citizens should be publicised as widely as possible and should also be submitted to legislatures in order to assist in scrutinising and monitoring departmental activities. Additionally, departments may utilise events such as open days (preferably not during working hours) to invite citizens to visit the department to meet with all levels of officials to discuss service delivery, standards, problems, etc.

Remedying mistakes and failures

The head of each department should regularly review complaints, and how they have been dealt with. Departments are required to review and improve their complaint systems, in line with the principles of accessibility, speed, fairness, confidentiality, responsiveness, review and training.

Getting the best possible value for money

All departments will be required, as part of their service delivery improvement programmes, to identify areas where efficiency savings will be sought, and the service delivery improvements that will result from achieving the savings.

Additional aspects

In addition to the principles, the document touches on various other aspects. These are discussed hereunder in an abbreviated form.

- *Improving innovation and rewarding excellence*: For *Batho Pele* to be successful, the commitment, energy and skills of public servants should be harnessed to tackle inefficient, outdated and bureaucratic practices, to simplify complex procedures, and to identify new and better ways of delivering services. It is also important that the efforts of personnel, both individuals and groups, who perform well in providing customer service, should be recognised and appropriately rewarded. Performance management procedures must in future include an assessment of the performance of individual members of staff in contributing to improving service to the public. Departments must also ensure that an environment conducive to the delivery of services is created to enhance the personnel's capacity to deliver good services.
- *Partnership with the wider community*: The White Paper argues that the public service cannot develop a truly service-oriented culture without the active participation of the wider community, including the private sector and citizens themselves. Therefore, *Batho Pele* will seek to establish partnerships with the wider community, in which business and industry, non-governmental organisations, community-based organisations, academic institutions and other bodies throughout the community can all play a part. For example, local businesses may assist in funding the publication of service standards or a telephone help-line, or they may sponsor a customer survey in a variety of official languages. They could also offer secondments and exchanges to public servants to broaden their experience. As part of their consultation exercises, departments must involve representatives

of the wider community in discussions about the future development of public services.

6.3.6 Making it happen

The White Paper required that service delivery campaigns be started immediately, i.e. in 1997. It stipulates what should be included in the 'Service Delivery Improvement Programme' and that this should be communicated throughout departments. This programme should be integrated with other departmental transformation priorities.

It is rightly stated that improving service delivery is a continuous, progressive process – not a one-off task. As standards are raised, so higher targets must be set. Implementing a service delivery improvement programme is then illustrated as an eight-step cycle, namely:

- Identify the customer.
- Establish the customer's needs and priorities.
- Establish the current service baseline.
- Identify the improvement gap.
- Set service standards.
- Gear up for delivery.
- Announce service standards.
- Monitor delivery against standards, and publish results.

6.3.7 Monitoring progress

In the case of central and provincial departments, the Department of Public Service and Administration acts in conjunction with the Public Service Commission to ensure that their progress in implementing *Batho Pele* is systematically monitored. The Department of Public Service and Administration evaluates the overall effectiveness of the *Batho Pele* initiative and submits reports to Parliament. Local authorities are required to adhere strictly to the principles of the *Batho Pele* initiative. Therefore, some similar monitoring mechanism would have to be set up by provincial governments.

6.4 Actual progress

During 2003, the South African Human Rights Commission submitted its fourth report to Parliament on economic and social rights. Of interest is the chapter covering the period between 2000 and 2002. The report stated:

Government policy and service delivery between 2000 and 2002 was not up to standard, inter alia as a result of mismanagement and a lack of skills. Therefore, the Government was unable to comply with the constitutional rights of South Africans to, inter alia, education and housing.

Some of the points made in the report were:

- There is a lack of resources and management skills in provinces. This has led to under-spending, corruption, lack of coordination between spheres of government and a lack of service delivery.
- The government must immediately implement the judgment of the Constitutional Court and supply mothers and babies who have HIV/AIDS with anti-retroviral drugs.
- All children under the age of 18 years must receive a government grant as a cushion against impoverishment. The grant to children under the age of 7 years is unconstitutional, as the Constitution defines children as younger than 18 years.
- Land reform has been dragging on for too long, and the budgeted amounts have not been spent. Up to 2000 only two per cent of land envisaged for distribution by the Department of Agriculture and Land Affairs had been redistributed. The government's goal was that by 1999 at least 30 per cent had to be redistributed. During the period 2000 to 2002 the Department of Agriculture and Land Affairs had failed to spend R128 million.
- A lack of financial skills is undermining children's right to education: 10 849 public schools did not have electric power; 13 204 did not have schoolbooks; and 10 723 had a shortage of classrooms.

Within Parliament itself, the government has agreed that the quality and quantity of public service delivery has not, as yet, produced the expected results. Perhaps the reason for this is, as Covey (1992:98) puts it, that we are locked into specific mind-sets or paradigms and locked into an outdated model of leadership, where the experts at the top, after consulting, decide the objectives, methods and means. In the course of the last few years the government has addressed these issues and has brought about improvement in some areas.

It seems that if planning were to be centred on an overall purpose or vision and on a commitment to a set of principles, such as *Batho Pele*, the people who are closest to the action could use their own expertise and judgment to make decisions and to take action.

The *Batho Pele* principles are not practices. As Covey (1992:98) puts it: 'Practices are specific activities or actions that work in one circumstance but not necessarily in another. If you manage by practices and lead by policies, your people don't have to be the experts, they don't have to exercise judgment, because all of the judgment and wisdom is provided them in the form of rules and regulations.' The idea is to focus on principles, thereby empowering everyone who understands those principles to act without constant monitoring, evaluating, correcting or controlling. Principles have universal application. When they are internalised into habits, they empower people to create a wide variety of practices to deal with different situations.

Managing by means of principles, as opposed to managing by means of plans and practices, requires a different kind of training and more intensive training. The reward is more expertise, creativity and shared responsibility at all levels of public service. When people are trained in the **practices** of public service delivery, we would get a degree of good service, but the service will break down, as it often does, whenever citizens (customers) present a special case or problem, because in doing so, they short-circuit standard operating procedures.

6.5 Benchmarking

The obvious debate in the situation in which South Africa finds itself, with its massive deficits and deficiencies in public goods and service delivery, is whether emphasis should be placed on the quantity or the quality of public services that need to be delivered. However, before one can address those aspects, there has to be an improvement in government as a whole. Benchmarking will improve government because it organises information to facilitate consistent improvement (Caplin and Dwyer, 2000:67). Benchmarks are used as a level of performance that a government aims to meet.

Benchmarks consist of two elements:

- **indicators** that measure a specific condition;
- **an objective** for that condition.

Benchmarking is an evaluative system designed to assist public officials to improve performance. Paraphrasing Osborne and Gaebler (1992), the benefits of evaluation are:

- What gets benchmarked gets done.

- If results are not benchmarked, one cannot tell success from failure.
- If success is not seen, one cannot learn from it.
- When one can demonstrate results, one can win support.

Obtaining a clear concept of the current situation and a future objective, in measurable terms, may create a target on which everyone can agree.

Caplin and Dwyer (2000:69) have created five general categories that are used in assessing government action:

- the cost of public services;
- the workload of public services;
- the efficiency of public services;
- the quality of public services;
- the quality of life in a community.

6.5.1 Indicators

Indicators may be described as clear descriptions of what governments do and how well they do it. An indicator may be qualitative, such as whether a department conducts accommodating customer reception, or quantitative, such as the per capita costs of police services in a given year.

Indicators become benchmarks when objectives are set. For example, when the objective is for a department to conduct accommodating customer reception, the benchmark would be 'conducting accommodating customer receptions', and when one wants the costs of police services to be no more than a desired average, that average becomes the benchmark.

Choosing benchmarks is a political way to communicate with citizens in order to establish what is important to them and what should be accomplished to improve society. In a democracy, citizens, elected and appointed officials and workers should openly exchange views on how they feel society should improve. That is so because benchmarking requires a clear statement of objectives and how they will be measured.

6.5.2 Objectives

Benchmarking forces one continually to keep the following questions in mind:

- **Objectives:** What needs to be accomplished?
- **Measurement:** How will one know if it has been done?

If these questions cannot be answered, one cannot benchmark. If they can be answered, the performance of government can be improved. Objectives in benchmarking are approximations that may be adjusted if they do not prove useful. It is important to start the process and to modify the objectives continuously as more information becomes available. Caplin and Dwyer (2000:75–77) give some guidelines to follow:

THREE WAYS TO SET OBJECTIVES

Method of analysis	Description	Example (police)
Absolute analysis	One has a level in mind	95 per cent of citizens say they feel safe when walking at night
Analysis over time	One wants it better than the previous year	Reduce the annual number of violent crimes by 10 per cent
Comparative analysis	One wants to be better than average	Clear more cases than the country's average

The absolute level method

The absolute level method is easy to understand and measure. However, choosing an absolute level can be arbitrary; when the highest level is chosen, it may be so far out of reach that it threatens credibility and defeats the purpose of setting benchmarks. Absolute levels may be based on arbitrary selection, such as 'the literacy level of South Africa should be 100 per cent'. The most useful approach is to have these levels ascertained by a government or a professional agency. The problem is that there are not enough standards for many public services. Also, many standards are open to question because they may be shaped by special interests.

The analysis over time method

This is more credible than the absolute level method and less costly than the comparative method. For example, one can plot the response time to police calls for a period of three to five years. If one is concerned about complaints in the assessor's office, one can call for a percentage reduction in the number of complaints from the previous year. However, if performance is very low, calling for a percentage increase may still leave a public service wanting by creating a benchmark that lets everyone off the hook. The method is credible because the existing performance is known and the direction in which it should move is clear. A possible threat to credibility may be controversy over how much improvement to pursue. This could be dealt with by reaching a compromise.

The comparative method

This method is usually useful in analysis over time. For example, the average performance of all municipalities in the country may be used as the basis for the benchmark. The mark could be set above, below or at average but the national average will be used as a source of measurement. Comparing across several units allows for ranking, and this way of using rankings creates an easily understood benchmark.

The downside of ranking is that it could force artificial competition and may backfire, especially if there is little variation in performance. For example, a municipality may have the lowest ranking, but by a difference of only two per cent when compared to the top municipality. Therefore, spending money to be the top municipality may not be useful. That is why using the average as the benchmark is generally preferable to ranking.

The most important disadvantage to the comparative approach is that it is time-consuming and costly to compile the information. When comparing a municipality with five or more others, data have to be collected on those other towns in order to find the average. Also, the use of comparison assumes incorrectly that one municipality is necessarily similar to the other municipalities used for the comparison. For example, municipalities with a lower per capita income will usually look worse when compared with those with richer populations.

6.5.3 Gaining and utilising information

Once the service to be measured has been identified, it will have to be determined whether the information is readily available or whether the data will have to be collected. Public records may be used, but a survey may have to be conducted.

The objective that has been set will determine what information has to be collected. When the absolute method is used, only information required for the current time period need to be collected. When the analysis over time method is used, information for at least the current year and previous years will be needed. When the comparative method is used, all the units in the sample will have to be collected.

However, gaining precise information on indicators is the most difficult, time-consuming and frustrating part of benchmarking. Accurate, reliable and comparable information is difficult to obtain, mainly for the following reasons:

- **Complications in analysis:** Creating useful indicators requires expertise and strenuous attention to detail.
- **Difficulty in obtaining data:** Few workers and managers rank keeping data on a systematic basis as a high priority.
- **Difficulty in making comparisons:** Governments collect indicators in different ways and for different periods.
- **Interpretation of statistics:** Small changes in the way indicators are collected and displayed can produce very different results.

The actual use of numbers such as percentages, rates and trend graphs is also problematic. Numbers can be manipulated to make the point one wants to make.

6.5.4 Benchmarking the costs of public services

An efficient government spends as little money as possible to reach the most beneficial results. The following issues need to be addressed when considering cost:

- the amount of work resulting from every rand spent;
- how completely the work is done;
- the impact of public services on society.

Public servants are constantly under pressure to reduce costs. Benchmarking may assist in communicating objectives for public expenditure. Caplin and Dwyer (2000:87) list the following steps for benchmarking public service costs:

- Step 1: Select the public service for which cost is an issue.
- Step 2: Decide whether to use analysis over time or comparative analysis.
- Step 3: Collect the appropriate data. For analysis over time, data on the particular unit (department or municipality) need to be

collected for different time periods. For comparative analysis, data are needed for at least four outside units (for example towns in the country) for the most recent year. Data for the past year may have to be averaged to account for uneven patterns.

- Step 4: Carefully scrutinise the data and charts.
- Step 5: The format to be used in public discussions and written reports will have to be selected. The comparative information should be borne in mind. Benchmarking is a way of thinking first and then a way of reporting.
- Step 6: It should be understood that cost information alone is not sufficient. The departmental workload, the quality of public service and the impact on the community should also be considered.

6.5.5 Benchmarking the workload of public services

Considering costs only can be dangerous. Reducing a highly valued service as part of a cost-saving effort may lead to public protest and government action. Therefore, costs based on the amount of work a government does are better than simple cost or workload information. Cost and workload information may be used to study the efficiency of public services, such as how much it costs for each service provided.

For example, it can be ascertained whether, say, a particular police station costs more than others in the country. For this, the analysis over time method as well as the comparative analysis method may be used. The analysis over time method requires only data collected from one station, and is therefore the easiest route. However, the comparative analysis method is often more useful than analysis over time when dealing with workloads. It makes more sense to compare one station with others than to compare a station with itself over time.

Caplin and Dwyer (2000:94) suggest the following steps for benchmarking the workload of public services:

- Step 1: Choose a workload measure based on the following criteria: It is related to the concern about cost that has already been benchmarked. It is thought that the station may be doing either too much or too little of something, or one may want to use the information as a point of reference
- Step 2: Decide whether to use analysis over time or comparative analysis.

- Step 3: Collect the appropriate data.
- Step 4: Study the data carefully and think about whether the information supports the original view. If the evidence suggests that there has been a decline in the number of, say, patrol units, and the community feels that crime is getting worse, one could use this type of information to support an increase in the number of patrol units.
- Step 5: Decide and keep in mind whether analysis over time or comparative analysis will be used in public discussions and written presentations.
- Step 6: It should be understood that workload information alone is not sufficient. If workload information is going to be related to costs and quality, it should be combined with other analyses.

6.5.6 Benchmarking the efficiency of public services

The type of benchmarking assists in answering the question, how much does each unit of public service cost and is this cost a good value? In order to answer this, one needs both cost information (such as annual expenditure) and workload information (such as total number of incidents). With these numbers one can find the average expense per incident by dividing the total expenditure by the number of incidents.

Workload costs generally represent efficiency, and indicate that the department has a workload appropriate to its expenditure. This knowledge could assist in controlling costs, yet this is not the final step towards benchmarking for better government. One also has to know the quality of service delivery (for example, police services) and the impact it has on the crime rate.

Comparative analysis for efficiency is more effective than analysis over time. As usual, in comparative analysis, the benchmark is set as the average. The department is efficient when it is performing below the mean, or average, expense per incident in the country. Departments could often display a perceived inefficiency rate: for example, province A may have a high cost per incident of crime because it has few incidents and spends a lot of money on prevention. Therefore, the total amount spent on policing may be similar to other departments, but the allocation may reduce the number of incidents.

Caplin and Dwyer (2000:99) suggest the following steps for benchmarking the efficiency of public services:

- Step 1: Select a public service about which the value of work performed is to be evaluated.
- Step 2: Decide whether to use analysis over time or comparative analysis.
- Step 3: Collect the appropriate data.
- Step 4: Review the data; for example, some departments may need to look at why their costs are so high compared to the amount of work they perform, or such information could stimulate communication between departments.
- Step 5: Decide whether analysis over time or comparative analysis will be most useful. They could be used for an in-house analysis or for public presentation.
- Step 6: Keep in mind that efficiency information on its own is not sufficient. The quality of services delivered and the impact on the community must also be considered.

6.5.7 Benchmarking the quality of public services

In business, quality is measured in three ways:

- company records that provide information on, say, the number of defects per thousand units or the durability of the product;
- customer surveys asking them to assess products and services;
- quality-assurance standards established by professional associations and public agencies.

Each approach has been used in assessing the quality of public services. In some cases, public records may be an important component of measurement: for example, how quickly the fire department responds to priority calls. Public records can be used for any type of service.

The most valuable approach to assessing the quality of public services is to ask recent users or receivers to comment on the quality of service. Customer surveys provide ideas about how to improve services. Benchmarking about continuous improvement and suggestions by citizens should be built into the effort. For example, respondents could be asked to comment on how prompt, courteous and thorough the police were in response to a homeowner who reported some unlawful act. Also, they could be asked what the police might have done differently.

The most feasible method of analysis for customer surveys is analysis over time. An absolute level, such as that the office should score a 10, using a 1–10 scale, is probably unrealistic. It may be more practical to consider an 8 or higher as the benchmark the personnel should strive to achieve. A customer survey is not a survey of the entire population. It is a survey of people who have used or received a service recently and of those who can make specific comments on the quality of the service.

All departments that provide direct services should use customer surveys. Once the results have been collected, the findings must be reported to elected officials, the respective departmental heads, the appropriate personnel and the public. Caplin and Dwyer (2000:106) suggest the following steps in benchmarking the quality of public services:

- Step 1: Select the public service that requires a quality study.
- Step 2: Decide what indicators to use: either *public records* or *customer surveys*.
- Step 3: Collect the appropriate data. If a customer survey is not being used on a regular basis, one should be designed and implemented.
- Step 4: the department needs to improve the quality of its service, carefully scrutinise the data to determine whether they support the initial conclusions.
- Step 5: Keep in mind that the quality of service must also be connected to the cost of service and the overall impact on the community's objectives. A department may be needed to meet the national standards set for the best departments, but it may not be feasible to spend the money to make the necessary changes.

6.5.8 Benchmarking the quality of life in the community

Governance would be easier if concerns only focused on the efficiency and quality of government services. Actually, some of the most pressing issues are related to society's quality of life. Among a broad spectrum of issues, the important one is whether the environment is pleasant, healthy and safe. Benchmarking is the key in the continuous pursuit of making communities better.

Collecting indicators on quality of life is costly because it requires data that departments usually do not keep. One has to understand the limited role of government in the pursuit of raising the quality of community life. Quality of life indicators are only partially affected by what governments do. The behaviour and attitude of the entire community, its physical setting and outside forces (such as the national economy) play a major role. For example, people who litter their streets are going to leave dirty streets despite the quality of rubbish removal. Benchmarking in this sense should be viewed as a mechanism for getting everyone responsible for the problems in the community to work together. This means building a coalition among public officials, non-governmental organisations, community-based organisations, business and citizens with the purpose of recognising a problem and agreeing on how each will assist in helping to solve it.

At the level of quality of life, one is concerned with the larger picture. This has to be kept in mind when making use of public records. For example, if one is reflecting on economic development in a province, the province's unemployment rate could be considered. If one is concerned about the health conditions in a city, one can consider morbidity and mortality rates.

The way in which people perceive their community is critical in raising quality of life and should be closely monitored through general population surveys. These surveys should be distinguished from customer surveys, which focus on individuals who have recently received a public service and ask them to assess its quality. General population surveys ask all members of a community for their reflections on a variety of societal conditions.

Another method to examine quality of life issues is direct observation. This means training individuals to observe conditions such as street litter and to complete forms correctly. Checks on the way observers complete the forms should be conducted on a systematic basis. In this regard, Caplin and Dwyer (2000:113–14) issue three warnings:

- Do not allow quality of life studies to be too broad and consume too many resources.
- Do not imply that the government holds primary responsibility for the quality of life in the community.
- Do not use benchmarks that are counterproductive.

Finally, Caplin and Dwyer (2000:115) suggest the following steps for benchmarking the community's quality of life:

- Step 1: Decide whether undertaking a quality of life study makes sense. Measuring the efficiency and quality of public services often provides sufficient information to make informed decisions.
- Step 2: Decide which method of quality of life analysis will be employed.

- Step 3: Ascertain whether public records are sufficient before undertaking a general population survey or direct observation.
- Step 4: There are six steps in general population surveys:
    1. Become familiar with an existing quality of life survey.
    2. Develop the survey.
    3. Test the survey.
    4. Decide how the survey will be distributed.
    5. Distribute the survey.
    6. Analyse the results and create the appropriate benchmarks.
- Step 5: There are six steps in the direct observation method:
    1. Use available direct observation studies as a model.
    2. Develop the direct observation form.
    3. Train the observers.
    4. Test the direct observation form and make the necessary changes.
    5. Conduct the direct observations
    6. Analyse the results and create the appropriate benchmarks.

6.6 Wrapping up

It is difficult to say whether the *Batho Pele* initiative has had any significant impact on improving and transforming service delivery. One could argue that many government departments (including those of local governments) had initiated delivery improvement schemes and programmes even before the publication of the White Paper. The national government itself has launched pilot studies in central and provincial government departments in order to demonstrate the feasibility of implementing such programmes. It is not yet certain whether that initiative was successful.

Although the national government has over the years launched various initiatives to improve overall public goods and service delivery, it has met with partial success. It is also a fact that in many departments and municipalities the *Batho Pele* principles are being strongly promoted. However, in practice too many citizens (as customers) are receiving poor public service delivery or are not receiving it at all. One way of implementing the principles could be through the processes of benchmarking.

PRINCIPLES, VALUES AND NORMS PRESENTED IN THIS CHAPTER

Strengthening constitutional democracy
Authority of institutions covers the values and principles of the Constitution
Action when public service is presumed or alleged to be improper or harmful
Promoting the protection, development and realisation of human rights
Promoting the protection of rights of cultural, religious and language communities
Promoting respect for and developing protection and realisation of gender equality
Auditing public accounts and reporting findings
Independent managing of elections
Regulating broadcasting in the public interest
Batho Pele to ensure better goods and service delivery
Consultation
Setting service standards
Ensuring public access
Ensuring courtesy
Providing information
Ensuring openness and transparency
Ensuring redress
Ensuring value for money in the delivery of goods and services
Improving innovation and rewarding excellence
Forming partnerships with the wider community

Having studied this chapter, how would you now answer the question posed at the beginning?
Find an article or a directive with *Batho Pele* as its theme, and analyse whether it does justice to the principles laid down by government

Chapter 7

Ubuntu

IN THIS CHAPTER

After reading this chapter, you should be able to:

- provide a definition of *Ubuntu*;
- understand the emphasis placed on the human aspect;
- outline Africa's achievements in the social and spiritual spheres;
- discuss a practical approach to life and work;
- analyse the concept of an infinite capacity for the pursuit of consensus and reconciliation;
- discuss the challenges of social revival;
- investigate the movement away from *Ubuntu*.

Before studying this chapter, see if you can answer the following question:

Is the philosophy of *Ubuntu* applicable to the South African public service?

Don't listen to what leaders say, it will ruin *Ubuntu*.

7.1 Introduction

Ubuntu is a comprehensive value system aimed at the ideal of being a good person. It is typical of African and specifically South African culture. It is the principle of caring for one another's wellbeing and a spirit of mutual support. In short, *Ubuntu* is an all-inclusive, deep-rooted African world-view which pursues the primary values of intense humanness, caring, sharing and compassion, and associated values, ensuring a happy and qualitative human community life in a family atmosphere and spirit.

7.2 *Ubuntu* defined

Ubuntu is about the art of being a human person (Broodryk, 2005:12). In this sense, it is an ideal of being a good person. However, this does not mean that all *Ubuntu* people are good, but people are trying to live out their *Ubuntu* values in the same way that religious people strive to be good. Its characteristics are, inter alia:

- the human experience of treating people with respect;
- humanness, which means that being human comprises values such as universal brotherhood and sharing, and treating and respecting others as human beings;
- a way of life contributing positively to sustaining the wellbeing of people, the community or society;
- A non-racial philosophy applicable to all people as human beings.

The concept of *Ubuntu* has become known the world over as being typical of African, and specifically South African, culture (Cilliers, 2008:1). Among other things, it has been described as an underpinning of the concept of an open society, a universal truth, a way of life, an expression of human dignity, African humanism, helpfulness, trust, respect, sharing, caring, unselfishness and community. A concise definition would be 'humanity' or 'humanness', and derived from the belief that everyone is a human being through others: 'I am because you are' (Ramose, 1999:49; Shutte, 1993:46, in Cilliers, 2008:1).

Ubuntu originated in pre-colonial African rural settings that operated with the moral values of caring and compassion within the community, and with people acting out these values through ceremonies and rituals (Cilliers, 2008:2). These ceremonies and rituals not only embodied morality, but also created identity. In Africa, the reality of becoming a person through others is constituted through these ceremonies, and specifically through initiation ceremonies: 'Before being incorporated into the body of persons through this route, one is regarded merely as an "it", i.e. not yet a person. Not all human beings are therefore persons' (Louw, 2002, in Cilliers, 2008:2).

Although *Ubuntu* has in a sense lost its connection with pre-colonial rural origins, it is still a popular notion in the context of the restructuring of post-apartheid South Africa (Van Binsbergen, 2003:437, in Cilliers, 2008:2). It has possibly found a wide range of ideological, economic and political usages. For example, in its White Paper on Welfare the South African government leans heavily on the notion of *Ubuntu* when it discusses nation-building, transformation and reconstruction of South African society:

> *Ubuntu is the principle of caring for each other's wellbeing ... and a spirit of mutual support ... Each individual's humanity is ideally expressed through his or her relationship with others and theirs in turn through recognition of the individual's humanity ... It also acknowledges the rights and responsibilities of every citizen in promoting individual and social wellbeing.*

The following descriptions of *Ubuntu* are given as recipes for a new universal world order (Koka, in Broodryk, 2005:13):

- a non-racial philosophy or value system according to which all people are regarded and treated as human beings;
- a philosophy of tolerance and compassion;
- a philosophical concept that accepts humankind is one whole, comprising various racial groups;
- a supreme goodness breathed into man, which transformed man into a living soul; a being called 'human', reflecting the image and likeness of God in man;
- a divine spark, which as soon as it was instilled in the human soul immediately transformed and elevated man into a distinctively different being endowed with intelligence and power of dominion over the rest of the created beings;
- the quality and dignity of the human personality.

In *Ubuntu*, the emphasis is placed on the human aspect, and teaches that the value, dignity, safety, welfare, health, beauty, love and development of the human being are to come first and should be prioritised before all other considerations, particularly in modern times, before economics, financial and political factors are taken into account. In essence, *Ubuntu* is African (Broodryk, 2005:12), in the sense that it is the art of being a human being; it is the ideal of being a good person.

Therefore, *Ubuntu* may be defined as an all-inclusive, deep-rooted African world-view that pursues the primary values of intense humanness, caring, sharing and compassion, and associated values, ensuring a happy and qualitative human community life in a family atmosphere and spirit.

Mbigi and Maree (2005:viii) hold that Africa's achievements and genius do not lie in technology, but rather in the spiritual and social spheres. They add that if Africa is going to enter and win in the global economic environment, it must draw on its social and spiritual heritage. Some of the positive social values listed by Mbigi and Maree (2005:14) are morality, dignity, performance enterprise, authority (know the truth), survival of self and the group and creativity. To these Broodryk (2005:15) adds basic values, such as not to steal, not to murder, not to do any harm or cause pain to others, not to lie, not to become angry, not to cause terror and to be faithful to loved ones.

It is evident that *Ubuntu* has become a buzz word. However, this does not detract from the fact that, through their understanding of *Ubuntu*, Africans could probably make a distinctively African contribution towards and within globalisation (Van Binsbergen, 2003:449, in Cilliers, 2008:3). It no longer functions in a narrow sense, but may contribute towards the enrichment of humanity as a whole. Cilliers (2008:3) stresses that *Ubuntu* is an expression of African epistemology: truth and therefore meaning is found primarily in *Ubuntu*, i.e. in communion with the other. Consequently, any attempt to find meaning in Africa will have to take *Ubuntu* seriously.

7.3 A practical philosophy

It is accepted that *Ubuntu* is a philosophy by which Africans generally live on a daily basis. It may be viewed as a practical approach to life and work that encompasses all human activities. Khanyile (in Broodryk, 2005:14) claims that *Ubuntu* is the common, spiritual ideal by which all Africans south of the Sahara give meaning to life and reality. Their concept of *Ubuntu* is usually described as the spiritual foundation of life.

Ancient African wisdom and the origin of moral *Ubuntu* date back to about 1500 BC, even before the origin of the Ten Commandments (Koka, in Broodryk, 2005:14). *Ubuntu* was then captured in the holy Netchar Maat, which was associated with seven cardinal virtues (or the key to human perfectibility), namely, truth, justice, propriety, harmony, balance, reciprocity and order. From these basic virtues of ancient African wisdom practical guidelines were deduced for correct daily living, such as:

- not to steal;
- not to murder;
- not to do any harm or cause harm to others;
- not to lie;
- not to become angry;
- not to cause terror;
- to be faithful to loved ones.

These guidelines were orally transferred from generation to generation. They taught Africans how to behave and were the basic moral laws of traditional African societies (Broodryk, in Broodryk, 2005:15). The following are practical examples of *Ubuntu* behaviour:

- the way one talks (good, positive words uttered in a relaxed, positive manner);
- the way one walks (relaxed, in an unstressed way);
- the way one smiles (in a friendly way, naturally, heartily and not by grinning);
- the way one treats others, especially elders, children and those in need;
- the way one greets (in a friendly way, and by hugging and inquiring extensively about the other's wellbeing);
- the way one practises moral values, such as caring, sharing, respect and compassion in daily life.

Actions that could be described as part of positive *Ubuntu* behaviour or living are deeds such as visiting the sick, extending condolences to a family who has lost a loved one, adopting an orphan as one's own child, providing food for the needy, assisting the aged and greeting others in a friendly and considerate way.

In corporate life, *Ubuntu* rests heavily on the family spirit. When all employees regard themselves as members of the extended family in the workplace, it shows that there is respect for the *Ubuntu* notion of brotherhood or personhood. In such an environment, everybody regards themselves as sisters and brothers of the same family. *Ubuntu* binds the phenomena of family and extended family approaches both in general life and in the sphere of management (Broodryk, 2005:16).

The principle of solidarity in *Ubuntu* is not an indefinable concept but a practical demand by human beings to experience unconditional respect, dignity and care from the relevant group, community or society. As a practical example, the way that trade unions operate in a spirit of oneness indicates the philosophical aspect of *Ubuntu* solidarity. Also, when considering the original meaning of democracy – from the Greek *demos* (people) and *krateo* (rule or authority) – it is clear that *Ubuntu* democracy likewise allows people at all levels, even at the lowest levels, to play a practical and meaningful role in the workplace and in the policy- and decision-making processes.

7.4 The search for consensus

African culture appears to have an almost infinite capacity for the pursuit of consensus and, in the process, reconciliation (Cilliers, 2008:3). For example, the African concept of *indaba* entails more than a mere meeting. It is dialogue directed at achieving consensus and, ultimately, reconciliation. At an *indaba* (which could take a long time) everyone has the right to express an opinion until they are able to say *simunye* (we are one).

However, this also has a dispiriting aspect, i.e. *Ubuntu* could degenerate into an oppressive conformity and blind loyalty to the group or community. Failure to conform may be met with harsh punitive measures (Cilliers, 2008:3). A lively debate towards attaining consensus could solidify into stifling conformity. Nevertheless, the challenge remains, that is, to affirm unity and at the same time to value and endorse diversity. Louw (in Cilliers, 2008:4) puts it eloquently as follows:

> Ubuntu *as an effort to reach agreement or consensus should thus not be confused with outmoded and suspect cravings for (an oppressive) universal sameness, often associated with so-called ideology or 'modernistic' attempts at the final resolution of differences … True* Ubuntu *takes plurality seriously. While it constitutes personhood through other persons, it appreciates the fact that 'other persons' are so called precisely because we can ultimately never quite 'stand in their shoes' or completely 'see through their eyes'.*

When the Ubuntist *reads 'solidarity' and 'consensus' s/he therefore also reads 'autonomy', and 'cooperation'.*

In order to achieve the consensus of *Ubuntu*, there is also a need for dialogue and mutual exposure, a genuine reciprocity in which we encounter the difference of the other's humanness, so as to inform and enrich our own. This reciprocal space is formed through a respect for the particularity, individuality and historicity of the other (Louw in Cilliers, 2008:4):

- **Particularity** requires that we accept and appreciate the other exactly as they are, not trying to alter, manipulate or recreate the other in our own image. In a certain sense, then, *Ubuntu* could mean that a human being is a human being through the otherness of other human beings. That implies that if we alter or attempt to alter or manipulate the otherness of the other, we ourselves end up by being someone other than ourselves. Cilliers (2008:4) stresses that we have to face the other unreservedly. Therefore, *Ubuntu* is the art of interfacing, of finding meaning within the space of interfacing.
- **Individuality** means that *Ubuntu* defines the individual in terms of relationships. It represents a kind of web of reciprocal relations. It, therefore, signifies that 'I participate, therefore I am'. In this understanding of *Ubuntu*, there is not the competitiveness that often characterises the Western search for meaning, but rather *shosholoza* or 'work as one' (Cilliers, 2008:5). The web of reciprocal relations implies a paradigm shift from solitary to solidarity, from independence to interdependence, and from individuality to community. However, *Ubuntu* strives to incorporate both relation and distance, both individuality and community. Nelson Mandela has remarked that there is nothing wrong with individuals enriching themselves, as long as this enrichment benefits society.
- In the reciprocal space of *Ubuntu* the **historicity** of the other is also recognised, i.e. accepting the fact that the other is in the process of becoming and is not a fixed entity that could be reduced to a static set of characteristics, behaviours or functions. The grammar of *Ubuntu* not only refers to 'being' and 'becoming' and of self-realisation through others, but also of the self-realisation of others.

It is a fact that *Ubuntu* has been romanticised or used to promote political or exclusivist positions that function as a kind of dismissive and popular ideology (Cilliers, 2008:6). It is easy to climb on the bandwagon of *Ubuntu*. However, it may be used or abused as a magic wand that has to lubricate society as a type of nation-saving design, glossing over or sidestepping real conflict (Van Binsbergen, in Cilliers, 2008:6). It may be used as a useful pacifier, but worst of all, it may be distorted, especially in the South African context to legitimate a new form of apartheid or ethnocracy or pigmentocracy, in which culture or race or ethnicity draws new, or redraws old, boundaries between the diversity of people that comprises South African society. As far as that is concerned, Mdluli (in Cilliers, 2008:6) claims that *Ubuntu* is being abused in the service of political and ideological aspirations: '… this concept has been reclaimed by the African bureaucratic bourgeoisie to legitimise its own hegemony in the political struggles.' This is contrary to the ideal of *Ubuntu*:

> *Viewed as a moral and political exhortation and an expression of hope for a better future, Ubuntu … creates a moral community, admission to which is not necessarily limited by biological ancestry, nationality, or actual place of residence. To participate in this moral community, therefore, is not a matter of birthright in the narrower parochial sense. If birthright comes in at all, it is the birthright of any member of the human species to express concern vis-à-vis the conditions under which her or his fellow humans must live, and to act on that basis.* (Van Binsbergen, in Cilliers, 2008:6).

South Africa's peaceful political transition in 1994 could be attributed, inter alia, to the African sense of *Ubuntu*. This brought an end to the era when people were stripped of their dignity and had to resort to *ubulwane* (animal-like behaviour) to uphold apartheid laws. Maphisa (in Cilliers, 2008:6) holds that the transition from an apartheid South Africa to a democracy was a rediscovery of *Ubuntu*.

7.5 *Ubuntu* and social survival

South Africa's current challenge is to build a new dimension of citizenship into the spirit of *Ubuntu*. That is the ability to live for one's country, the ability to be personally responsible and accountable for improving one's situation

(Mbigi & Maree, 2005:vi). This is perhaps the missing link and dimension of *Ubuntu* in post-independence South Africa. Should the solidarity principle of *Ubuntu* be to survive beyond the fight for liberation, it must become dynamic and go through transformation to add the important dimension of citizenship and personal stewardship.

It is important not to marginalise the solidarity spirit of *Ubuntu* in present-day South Africa. Mbigi and Maree (2005:2) are of the opinion that South Africans should try to build on the collective spirit of *Ubuntu* and harness it for productivity and competitive purposes. At a national level, it should be harnessed in order to manage the challenges of reconstruction and development. A new inclusive national vision is needed, and *Ubuntu* may serve as a starting point for building this collective national vision. *Ubuntu* could assist organisations to develop corporate citizenship. By building the solidarity spirit of *Ubuntu*, it is possible to build cooperation and competitive strategies by allowing teamwork to permeate the whole organisation. It would also help South Africans to find a new identity as a nation – an identity that would transcend ethnic divisions.

The spirit of *Ubuntu* may help define a new critical path towards the present South Africa. If institutions are going to be productive, they will need to develop a tradition of working together on survival and competitive issues. The process should draw on the collective experience of black people in South Africa, and needs to be built on it. The proposal made by Mbigi and Maree (2005:3) is that South Africans need an innovative way to manage in the new South Africa, based on their collective experience and the lessons they have learnt. The new way should be a package of solutions to address the survival challenges of global competition, as well as reconstruction and development.

That approach will also have to incorporate the global experience of other developing countries. One of the many impediments facing developing countries is the lack of sufficient numbers of experienced and skilled managers, a situation that often leads to maladministration and mismanagement. The reliance on the West as the only model for managerial practice and development may be too limited. Mbigi and Maree (2005) stress that they are not suggesting that the Western experience should be neglected but that the point of departure should be to harness the South African collective cultural experience and then synthesise it with recent experiences from other developing countries, such as those in Asia and Latin America. They call for a celebration of global citizenship where everybody can be both tribal and cosmopolitan.

The plea by Mbigi and Maree (2005:4) is for a new developmental approach to management in South Africa. Managers cannot ignore the reality of underdevelopment in society. The approach should be based on collective solidarity and teamwork, but focusing on the developmental challenges that could be the survival answer for South African institutions. The developmental approach must focus on reframing people's minds and issues related to restructuring of society and institutions, renewing the spirit and morale of people and revamping processes and practices. This may assist institutions to be productive and engage in solving the problems of development and corporate renewal.

7.6 Movement away from *Ubuntu*

The opposite of *Ubuntu* could be called *Into*, which literally means 'a thing' (Cilliers, 2008:7). In African culture, certain initiation rituals embody the metamorphosis from being an 'it' (not yet a person) into being a member of society; of being a person within humanity. The opposite is also true: once people become severed from the community, or distance themselves from it, they no longer belong to humanity, and in a sense become a thing without humanness. In this respect, Cilliers argues that South Africa is going through such a movement in which people often treat one another as things and not as human beings.

The phenomenon of treating fellow human beings as inferior is nothing new. Under apartheid, different forms of dehumanisation were practised and actually legitimised. However, certain phenomena in contemporary South Africa may also be viewed from this perspective: for example, the alarming statistics of violent crime, with accounts of horrendous brutality, and tens of thousands of murders per annum; the stigmatisation flowing from HIV and AIDS; and xenophobic attacks. Xenophobia is the exact opposite of *Ubuntu*. In *Ubuntu* we face each other; in xenophobia, we turn our faces from each other. In addition, in xenophobia, the fear for the other becomes hatred for one another, and in the end, the ravaging of the other. It is *Into* in action, on a huge and devastating scale (Cilliers, 2008:9).

It is difficult to understand the perversities taking place in South African society, renowned for its spirit of *Ubuntu*. Perhaps the devastating impact of apartheid on society, even to the present, has been underestimated (Cilliers, 2008:11). Perhaps racism was not buried deep enough, and now its resurrection can be seen everywhere. Three hundred years of racism cannot be erased within a span of fifteen years. Cilliers comments that perhaps South Africans have misused the notion of *Ubuntu*, also pursued by the Truth and Reconciliation Commission, as a premature pacifier, which has the ultimate effect of creating a spirit of denial.

Whatever the reasons for all of this are, Cilliers (2008:12) believes that South Africans need to revisit the basic truths of *Ubuntu*: for example, the call for real dialogue and openness towards one another. From a religious perspective Cilliers believes that if preaching were to find meaning that makes a difference in South Africa, it must contribute towards the restoration of *Ubuntu* as humanness, as humanity towards humans. It will have to raise a voice against all forms of *Into*.

PRINCIPLES, VALUES AND NORMS PRESENTED IN THIS CHAPTER

Respect
Universal brotherhood
Wellbeing
Non-racialism
Humanness
Tolerance
Compassion
Goodness
Dignity
Morality
Performance enterprise
Truth
Survival of self and group
Creativity
Not to steal
Not to murder
Not to become angry
Not to cause terror

Faithfulness to loved ones
Solidarity
Consensus and reconciliation
New dimension of citizenship

Having studied this chapter, how would you now answer the question posed at the beginning?
In your own words, relate how the philosophy of *Ubuntu* could benefit the South African public service.

Chapter 8

Constitutional basis of managing public financial and human resources

IN THIS CHAPTER

After reading this chapter, you should be able to:

- explain the democratic principles of public financial management;
- define graft, bribery and corruption;
- define accountability and public accountability;
- discuss the context of managing public human resources;
- explain the concept of organisational culture;
- discuss codes of conduct;
- discuss the importance of standards of conduct in the public service;
- explain the function and importance of a code of ethics;
- explain some of the advantages and disadvantages of affirmative action;
- formulate a definition of nepotism;
- formulate a definition of racism.

Before studying this chapter, see if you can answer the following question:

Are you familiar with the terms discussed in this chapter?

Public money and parastatals seem to be incompatible.

8.1 Introduction

In order to deliver public goods and services, elected and appointed public officials have public resources at their disposal. These include, inter alia, natural, human, financial and information resources. The two most important of these, i.e. financial and human resources, are included in this chapter because they are pertinently dealt with in the Constitution.

8.2 Democratic principles for public financial management

In South Africa's form of representative democracy, public financial matters are decided by the representatives of the voters and taxpayers in the three spheres of government. Gildenhuys (in Schwella *et al*, 1996:133) asserts that, in this system, voters and taxpayers become spectators, in contrast to a participatory democracy where they are active participants. There is a strong possibility that the interests and preferences of taxpayers and the median voter could differ from those of their elected representatives. Therefore, the financial decisions made by representatives could conflict with the wishes of those voters whose interests they represent.

The South African Constitution, in Chapter 13, protects the interests of taxpayers (which means all citizens) and voters by providing for a National

Revenue Fund into which all moneys – mostly tax receipts – received by the national government have to be paid, except revenue reasonably excluded by an Act of Parliament. Money may be withdrawn from the National Revenue Fund only as provided by an Act of Parliament and as a direct charge against the Fund when such a provision is made in the Constitution or an Act of Parliament. The equitable share of the revenue collected nationally constitutes a direct charge against the National Revenue Fund. Provincial treasuries have also been established by the Constitution, and the fiscal affairs of local governments have been established by the Constitution and constitutionally based legislation.

In terms of an Act of Parliament, a National Treasury was established and measures introduced in order to ensure both transparency and control of expenditure in all spheres of government. In cases of serious and continuous contravention of these measures and with the approval of the national Minister of Finance and eventual consent of Parliament, the Treasury may refuse to transfer funds to an organ of state. A time limit and procedure is prescribed to resolve the matter. Furthermore, when an organ of state in the national, provincial and local spheres of government or any other institution identified in national legislation contracts for goods and services, it has to be done in terms of a system that is impartial, fair, transparent, competitive and cost-effective.

In any democracy, conflict between various stakeholders in public financial matters will always be present (Gildenhuys, 1993:54–60). The real conflict is between a variety of collective needs, competing for public resources, and which cannot all be satisfied. Decision-making should be aimed at obtaining a satisfactory solution to this conflict. The objective of reconciliation in the conflict is aimed at satisfying, through a democratic decision-making process, the optimum collective needs of society and to promote the equitable allocation of scarce resources among the competing collective needs, as well as the equitable distribution of the financial burden. The following may be identified as democratic values that could serve as basic principles in public financial and human resource management:

- Public resource decision-making should always aim at the most *reasonable* and *equitable* way in which public resources are allocated, as well as at the most *efficient* and *effective* way in which public resources can be applied to satisfy the collective needs of the public.
- The utilisation of public resources must satisfy collective public needs *optimally*.

- The utilisation of public resources is based on the principles of participatory democracy, i.e. *direct* or *indirect participation* by citizens, and consumers and users of public services, in the public decision-making process. This is a primary requirement for democratic public decision-making.
- No tax or other charges may be collected from the public without their consent, and this tax obligation must be distributed in a *reasonable* and *equitable* way.
- Only the collective body of elected political representatives has the authority to introduce taxes, to collect them and to decide how and on what they should be expended. It is because of this principle that the legislature (national, regional or local council) should not delegate its financial decision-making authority to an executive council. The principle in law of *delegatus non potest delegare* (someone with delegated authority may not further delegate that authority) is applicable.
- The elected political representatives are *responsible* and *accountable* to the public for the collection and spending of taxes and the utilisation of other resources.
- Political representatives must be *sensitive* and *responsive* to the collective needs of citizens. They must regard themselves as responsible for solving the public's collective problems and satisfying their collective needs. This is possible only when there is regular and free interaction between political representatives and the public.
- Executive authorities are responsible for efficient and effective policy and programme execution. Efficiency and effectiveness in an open democratic system mean that the execution of budget and policy programmes should satisfy the public needs, not only as cost-effectively as possible but also as extensively as possible.
- In a true democracy, the principle of *social equity* is extremely important. The outstanding feature of the concept is the maintenance of high ethical and moral standards, and this requires political representatives and public officials to act with integrity. In turn, integrity requires fairness, reasonableness and honesty in dealing with the public. In this way, public authorities are acting within both the letter and the spirit of the law, in the sense that they will be engaged in more than unethical conduct. Social equity requires the support and maintenance of the principles of democracy. This means that when

public policies are determined and public decisions are made, neither the interests of one group should be harmed nor the interests of another group be advanced undeservedly, or to the detriment of other groups.
- One of the cardinal values of democracy is that all activities regarding public management and administration *must take place in public, or must be transparent*, and not under the guise of secrecy or confidentiality. This principle requires that account should be given in public of all public matters. Matters excluded are, for example, those affecting national security.

8.3 Graft, bribery and corruption

The term 'graft' is seldom used today in relation to public affairs. In its original usage, it referred to gaining some kind of advantage in business and politics through bribery, unfair influence or other shady means, or a bribe and bribery used in this way. The term 'bribery' is understood to mean the process of offering money, gifts or favours to someone to commit an unlawful or dishonest deed to that person's advantage. Another term often used in cases of misdemeanours in the public sector is fraud, which is an act of deception and in most cases involves an intentional misrepresentation of resources (especially money) received and utilised.

Situations that occur in public services are those of mismanagement and maladministration, which simply means bad or incorrect management or administration. This can take many forms, from public servants not performing their duties at all to them not performing in terms of their contracts of employment. There are a variety of reasons for this, including idleness, incompetence, and contravening or deliberately ignoring the appropriate rules, regulations and legislation. The result is that the citizens of the country do not receive the public goods and services to which they are entitled.

The term '*corrupt*' refers to a condition of mental depravity that, inter alia, presents itself in acts of immorality and dishonesty. The term '*corruption*' refers to an act of being corrupt and corrupting someone else. Therefore, in the process of corruption two parties are involved: those offering money, gifts or favours with a view to obtaining an immoral, dishonest and unlawful advantage, and those who accept and act in the arranged way. Corruption is defined as a lack of personal honesty, especially of being susceptible to bribery, as well as the use of a position of trust for dishonest gain. It may also refer to subversion, i.e. destroying someone's honesty or loyalty, or undermining moral integrity. Finally, it may be defined as inducement by, for example a public official, by improper means, such as bribery, to violate duty.

Corruption plays a large role in politics and public administration. Citizens who have to receive public goods and services are sometimes seen by many elected and appointed public officials as major obstacles in their quest for enrichment. It is often difficult to discern between *need-driven* and *greed-driven* corruption when, for example, much-needed government contracts are at stake. Therefore, the process of planned democratic change and economic growth promises remains largely unfulfilled.

The media's preoccupation with corruption is understandable because it is a marketable commodity and they understand the public's fascination of seeing prominent personalities in embarrassing situations. Increasing public interest and concern over corruption has led to considerable scholarly research into the subject. Corruption is usually kept secret and remains difficult to observe in real life. It is the type of action where two or more actors broker an agreement or exchange relations by way of a successful transfer of material goods like money for favours (political or status) or enrichment, which sidesteps legality or civility to regulate the relationship. It is a strategic interaction or an art of negotiation. This type of social action is strategic when it is the successful realisation of personally defined goals and objectives.

The concentration of ill-gotten wealth in the hands of a few causes a distorted consumption pattern. Other people learn this pattern of favour-giving and favour-seeking by imitation. This underlies many other crimes and dishonest action, such as the misappropriation of public funds, remuneration for tasks not performed, fraud, nepotism, dereliction of duties and mismanagement and maladministration.

As a result of constitutional democracy and an open society, South Africans have become more and more aware of the deep-rooted culture of corruption threatening all aspects of social life in South Africa. In the political sphere, the media frequently report on real and alleged cases of corruption. The national government has, over the past years, appointed commissions of inquiry and task teams at all levels and in all spheres to investigate cases of fraud, corruption, mismanagement and maladministration. As one example, in 2002 the national government appointed a task team to investigate all forms of corruption in the national housing subsidy scheme and to ensure that the perpetrators were brought to book. Housing is a key area in which government has undertaken to perform.

The report of the task team included the following warnings, an indication that such offences were indeed committed:

- It is illegal for women to be requested to provide sexual favours before they may obtain a house.
- It is a serious offence for individuals not qualifying for a housing subsidy to access the subsidy.
- Individuals accessing more than one subsidy and the officials or councillors who assist them will be prosecuted as conspirators to the illegal act.
- People should not exchange government-subsidised housing without following the prescribed requirements.

When the investigation began, about a hundred cases in several provinces were identified as a priority. Out of those, 26 were urgently investigated by the task team, which found prima facie evidence of fraud and corruption. These cases were handed to the National Director of Public Prosecutions for further investigation and prosecution.

During the forensic audit conducted by the task team, it was revealed that R126 million was involved in cases such as the following:

- claims by contractors for subsidies for houses that were not built;
- cases of developers awarding subsidised houses to themselves and claiming the subsidies on the basis that the houses had been allocated to the intended beneficiaries;
- disregarding or failing to follow the necessary procurement procedures, including not following tender procedures, and awarding building contracts to suppliers of building materials who are not registered with the National Home Builders Registration Council and are therefore not authorised;
- irregular payments and false letters of appreciation;
- sale of subsidised houses to beneficiaries by officials and people pretending to represent government;

These cases involved contractors and developers, officials from regional and local government structures, including housing boards as well as civic leaders. This indicates, in only one area of government, the depth and breadth of the challenge faced by the country.

8.4 Accountability

The term 'accountability' has already been referred to on a number of occasions. A traditional cornerstone of democracy, especially where public money is concerned, is the fact that every elected and appointed public official is subject to what is known as accountability (see Schwella *et al*, 1996:164–167). Public accountability may be viewed from different points of view:

- Firstly, accountability is the responsibility of a government and its agents towards the public to achieve previously set goals and objectives and to account for them in public.
- Secondly, it is the commitment required from public officials individually and collectively to accept public responsibility for their actions (and inaction).
- Thirdly, it is the understood obligation of subordinates active in the public sector to keep their superiors informed of their execution of duties.

Public accountability is an important requirement in public and development management and has for many centuries been a central issue in the practice of public resource management. Elected and appointed officials alike are held responsible and accountable for the public resources placed under their control. In democratic government and administration, responsibility means that political representatives and public officials must account to citizens for the way in which public resources have been collected and procured, kept safe, and expended and utilised.

The difference between responsibility and accountability becomes clear when the issue of accountability is raised. The primary connotations of accountability, i.e. accountability as a responsibility, as the cause and as an obligation, as well as public accountability, are important where this cornerstone of democracy is considered. The connotations of accountability are discussed below.

8.4.1 Accountability as a responsibility

Individuals are responsible to their principals for the efficient, effective and responsive execution of assignments and performance of their duties, to the extent that they are, for the purpose of assignments and duties, under the control and command of other persons and institutions. Therefore, it may be concluded that those public institutions and persons responsible for the control, management and administration of public resources are accountable to the public at large for the efficient, effective and responsive execution of their assigned duties.

8.4.2 Accountability as the cause

Accountability may also refer to the cause of an event. Somebody may, because of his or her personal conduct, be responsible for the success of failure of a programme (an event). When someone is held responsible for a specific event, it is generally accepted that she or he also caused such an event. In some situations, a person, in terms of her or his responsibilities, may be held accountable without directly being the cause of the event.

In public affairs, accounting officers (e.g. a director-general) are responsible for the effective, efficient and responsive management of their institutions, and they should, typically, be responsible to the executive authority (e.g. Cabinet) and the legislature (e.g. select committee of Parliament) as representatives of citizens. In turn, the executive authority is obliged to give account to the legislature of any mismanagement and maladministration of public resources. The legislature itself and its members are directly responsible to the public at large and have to account to them for all activities, including cases of mismanagement and maladministration.

8.4.3 Accountability as an obligation

Accounting officers of public units are responsible for the effective, efficient and responsive management of the public resources entrusted to those units. This implies that they have an obligation to ensure that the resource management of their units is indeed effective, efficient and responsive. Also, the officers concerned are obliged to render account to higher authorities in this respect, and they cannot be exempted from any malpractices, nor may they place any blame on anyone else.

8.4.4 Public accountability

Public accountability is the obligation resting on all public functionaries to act in the public interest and according to their conscience, with solutions for all matters based on professionalism and participation, with divulgement as a safety measure. This is a natural consequence and an essential safeguard against the abuse of power; the delegation of authority also means a delegation of accountability.

The concept of accountability on its own does not necessarily imply public accountability. Public accountability goes hand in hand with representative democracy and its associated rights and privileges of citizens and obligations for political representative and public officials. Public accountability as such does not necessarily imply that accountability towards the public enjoys universal acceptance. Public officials in totalitarian or elite systems may not be held accountable, while in others they may be held even more accountable than some of their counterparts in representative democracies, as they may, in a disciplined hierarchical structure, be held directly accountable to an authoritarian head of state, and to her or him alone. However, this hierarchical accountability does not operate in public but in private.

Accountability may be placed in direct contrast to bureaucratic and hierarchical accountability. Public accountability is normally associated with Western democracies. It requires making all facts public, so that public debate may be conducted on those facts. The debate should be accessible to both politicians and the public. Basic to the debate on public resources is acceptance of the fact that the public, as taxpayers, do not only have obligations but defined rights as well. Also, it is based on the principle of the sovereignty of the public at large over the financing of government activities. Public accountability is also the instrument by which political representatives as a body (national, regional and local council) established and expanded their control over public resources. Real public accountability implies that those responsible should also report to other parties, including the public, and not only to their political parties and their immediate authorities in the hierarchy of government.

The essential value of public accountability is that elected political representatives and public officials are required to conduct public dialogue among themselves on what they are doing and intend to do, and on the suppositions on which their activities are based. The most important supposition is that secrecy in public resource management conceals maladministration, mismanagement and corruption.

The ethical base of public accountability is the accord created between government authority and the government's accountability to the public. Official activities should not only receive negative criticism; effective, efficient and responsive public management should be made public in a positive way. The true function of public accountability should not be to focus on negative aspects only, but also to view it as a curative instrument by means of which shortcomings may be identified in advance, so that curative action may be taken to prevent maladministration, mismanagement and corruption. It should also focus on the positive aspects so that they may serve as examples of good governance.

The fundamental premise is that all public institutions financed from public funds are held responsible and have to account in public for the honest, effective, efficient and responsive expenditure of public funds and other resources. Therefore, public accountability cannot be aimed solely at the internally audited correctness of public records. The point of departure of public accountability has moved away from an attempt to control public officials exactingly within a structure of financial discipline, represented by a strong central entity, to a more positive approach of evaluating the results of the activities of public institutions for effectiveness, efficiency and responsiveness. Although this evaluation is directed at a positive contribution to prevent wastage of public resources, it does not imply that strict discipline in this regard should be disregarded.

The conclusion to be drawn from this analysis is that representative democracy stresses the need for the public accountability of both political representatives and public officials. This implies that account should be given in public, and it places an obligation on each elected and appointed official to act in a responsible way and in the interests of every member of society. Compliance with the principle of accountability is not a simple matter, as borne out in the case described below.

In March 2006, the Standing Committee on Public Accounts (SCOPA) of the South African Parliament met (refer to www.pmg.org.za/node/7376). The meeting was aimed at establishing the compliance of public entities with the Public Finance Management Act (PFMA). In summary, information was provided on the status of Telkom (the telecommunications parastatal) with regard to reporting requirements. Discussions touched on insider trading, which had to be avoided, and all stakeholders had to receive pertinent information. It was also felt that oversight should be improved in the public sector. Capacity-building programmes would be introduced to support compliance. An interface with all role-players was suggested.

It is interesting that the public interest, as entrenched in the Constitution – for example, values such as transparency and the role of Parliament as the representative of the country's citizens – was not a priority in the discussions of the committee. Telkom is a public entity, and is maintained by South African society. In answer to certain questions, the official answers were as follows:

> *The Chief Director: Asset Management stated that the government owned 37 per cent of Telkom, which actually means that the South African public owns that share. The government (representing the public) held a voting bloc and could appoint the Board and vote at the Annual General Meeting. However, the government could not instruct Telkom to operate in the broader public good ... National Treasury recommended that SCOPA interrogate all financial statements emanating from Telkom and fulfil an oversight function.*
>
> *A member confirmed that SCOPA played an oversight role and asked whether the Department of Communications (DOC) held the shares on behalf of the government. He asked whether the Auditor-General had a role to play regarding Telkom, given that the entity had removed itself from the auspices of PFMA. It was confirmed that DOC served as the principal shareholder on behalf of government.*
>
> *The Chairperson asserted that the Committee's priority was to ensure that no public entity existed that did not account to Parliament. The listing of Telkom surrendered Parliament's right of oversight. The Committee had to ensure that adequate levels of accountability were maintained and public resources were spent in an acceptable manner.*

8.5 Public human resources

The South African Constitution, in Chapter 10, defines the way in which human resources in the public service should be managed, i.e. by the democratic values and principles enshrined in the Constitution. As pointed out, the following principles apply to the administration in all spheres of government, organs of state and public enterprises:

- A high standard of professional ethics must be maintained and promoted.
- Effective, efficient and economic use of public resources must be promoted.
- The public service must be development-oriented.
- Public goods and services must be delivered impartially, fairly, equitably and without bias.

- The public service must be responsive to the needs of the people, and the public must be encouraged to participate in policy-making.
- The public service must be accountable.
- Transparency must be advanced by providing the public with timely, accessible and accurate information.
- Sound human-resource and career-development practices, to maximise human potential, must be cultivated.
- The public service must be broadly representative of South African society, with employment and human resource management practices based on ability, objectivity, fairness and the need to redress the imbalances of the past in order to achieve broader representation.

Besides these principles, there are certain trends, opportunities and threats stemming from the external environment. Elected and appointed public officials should identify and act upon these trends to be successful. Also, the political environment and its direct link with political structures have a direct impact on the public service, and are constantly being influenced by political factors. National political structures, including political parties, interest and pressure groups and the public at large are involved in the process of policy-making, and these trends have to be identified and analysed.

Public human resource management is greatly affected and influenced by legislation. Laws are legally binding, authoritative norms with which people have to comply. They include the rules of administrative, and common and customary law. Enforceable regulations, Acts, ordinances and by-laws passed by competent and authoritative rule-making institutions in the legislative, executive and administrative branches of government constitute the body of statutory law.

8.6 Organisational culture

An organisation's culture conveys to employees and observers the way in which the organisation functions (see Fox, 2006:32–40). It is a relatively uniform perception of the organisation, and is shared by its members. 'Culture' is a descriptive rather than an evaluative concept. An organisation's culture represents common and stable attributes that distinguish one organisation from another.

Individuals with different backgrounds or at different levels within the organisation tend to describe the organisation's culture in similar terms. Research has found that they perceive a unique set of characteristics that are specifically organisation-specific. Researchers have identified seven characteristics as distinctive to an organisation's culture:

- **Conflict tolerance:** the degree of conflict in relationships between peers and work groups, and also the willingness to be open and honest about differences.
- **Identity:** the degree to which members identify with the organisation as a whole rather than with a work group or field of professional expertise.
- **Individual autonomy:** the degree of independence, responsibility and opportunity that individuals have for exercising initiative.
- **Performance reward:** the degree to which reward allocations are based on employee performance criteria.
- **Risk tolerance:** the degree to which employees are encouraged to be vigorous, innovative and risk-seeking.
- **Structure:** the degree of rules and regulations and amount of direct supervision used in overseeing and controlling employee behaviour.
- **Support:** the degree of assistance and mutual regard provided by managers to their subordinates.

Each of these characteristics exists on a continuum from low to high. By appraising an organisation on these characteristics, a composite picture of that organisation may be formed. As organisational culture is a descriptive term, it is concerned with employee perception of the characteristics and not whether they like them or not. In terms of culture, one organisation may be distinguished from another.

8.6.1 Culture and functioning organisations

Organisational culture is the social adhesive that assists in holding the organisation together by providing standards about what employees should say and do. It proposes a consummate plan through which employees can understand what attitudes and behaviours are preferred. It also creates norms that act to shape the behaviour of individuals as well as groups within the organisation.

An organisation's culture has an influence on who are offered jobs and whether candidates accept offers. This means that candidates are assessed as to whether their attitudes and behaviours are compatible with the culture. It also means that candidates attempt to assess the organisation to determine whether they would find the work environment comfortable and beneficial.

8.6.2 The roots of culture

An organisation's culture should, in practice, be the result of its history, environment, selection process and socialisation practices.

Organisations have histories. An organisation's prevailing beliefs, customs, traditions and ways of doing things are essentially due to what it has done in the past and the degree of success it had with those endeavours.

An organisation has to satisfy the requirements of the critical constituencies within its **environment**, upon which it depends for support. Its environment defines its strategy and what it has to do in order to be successful. Indirectly, then, the environment is a significant force in shaping an organisation's culture.

Its **selection** process influences an organisation's culture. Organisations do not employ everyone who applies. Selection decisions include judgments as to whether a candidate will fit into the organisation. This attempt to ensure a suitable match contributes towards the creation of a uniform culture within the organisation.

An organisation's **socialisation** process for new employees is the major mechanism for culture indoctrination. A new employee is unfamiliar with the organisation's culture and is likely to disturb the values, norms and customs that are in place when she or he enters the organisation. Therefore, new employees are processed in order to get them to adapt to the organisation's culture. This process of adaptation is called socialisation, and usually consists of orientation or training programmes. These programmes may be formal or informal; individual or collective; over a fixed or variable time limit; serial or disjunctive; or investiture or divestiture:

- *Informal* socialisation takes place on the job, and the new member gets little or no attention. In *formal* socialisation, in contrast, the new member, in varying degrees, is segregated from the ongoing work setting and differentiated in some way to make clear her or his newcomer's role. The more formal the programme, the more likely it is that the new member will experience the learning that management desires. Informal socialisation will increase the influence of the immediate work group on the new member.

- *Individual* socialisation is likely to develop less homogeneous views than *collective* socialisation. As with informal structure, individual socialisation tends to preserve individual differences and perspectives.
- A *fixed* schedule reduces uncertainty for the new member, as transition is standardised. In contrast, *variable* schedules give no advance notice of their transition timetable, and characterise the schedule for most professionals and managerial personnel.
- In *serial* socialisation, an experienced member guides or directs the new member and, therefore, acts as a tutor or model for the new member. When the new member has no predecessors to guide her or him or on which to model her or his behaviour, it is called *disjunctive* socialisation. Serial socialisation maintains traditions and customs, while disjunctive socialisation tends to create more inventive and creative employees because new members are not burdened by traditions.
- *Investiture* practices confirm the usefulness of the characteristics that a person brings to a new job. Individuals have been selected on the basis of what they can bring to the job, and the organisation does not want to change them. Entry is made as smooth and trouble-free as possible. In this case, socialisation efforts are aimed at reinforcing the reasons why a person was employed in the first place. In *divestiture* socialisation there is the desire to strip away certain entering characteristics of a new member. For example, the selection process identified the candidate as a potential high performer. Now it is necessary to make such minor modifications that will improve the fit between the new member and the organisation.

8.6.3 Investigating organisational culture

During 2000 a tool was developed whereby values in an organisation, such as a public service organisation, could be measured (see Schwella *et al*, 1996:35). The accuracy of measuring orientation towards a specific value by means of a single question may pose a problem. However, the value lies within the use of value clusters as a measurement to determine orientation. An additional value may be found in the use of a single tool for longitudinal comparisons. This tool was effectively used in 2000, 2003 and 2004, and this section focuses on the research findings of 2003.

A large government department was selected in which the research was conducted. Values that indicate the state of the organisational culture were chosen. Some of the findings indicated a positive association with the value clusters of professionalism, commitment to excellence and the maintenance of discipline. This should be regarded as a positive indication. Half or less of the entire sample indicated a negative perception towards the value cluster supervisors/leaders' fulfilment of human dignity and loyalty to the department.

Regarding orientation towards individual values, the values expected of efficient service delivery, such as organisational competence, ethics, discipline, acceptance of authority, courage, teamwork, obedience and self-discipline, indicated a high association. However, other values, such as loyalty, pride in the department and discrimination, showed low association.

The system that was developed tested values during July to August 2000 by means of a survey among members of the department, using a self-administered, structured omnibus questionnaire. The survey was repeated during September 2003. The focus here is on the respondents' degree of association with the proposed value system of the department.

8.6.4 Sampling

The population of the study was defined as certain members of the department. A computerised multi-stage sampling procedure, consisting of stratified, systematic and random sampling techniques, was used to identify prospective participants. The variables of service/division, rank group, gender, former employment and population group were used. The field work was done in all nine provinces of South Africa. A total of 2 277 completed questionnaires were received.

The comparison of the sample with the actual population by means of the characteristics of the five above-mentioned variables indicates a fairly representative sample.

8.6.5 Data analysis

Descriptive statistical techniques were used to analyse the data, namely, frequencies, cross-tabulations and percentages. The focus fell on broad value clusters (factors) comprising a group of questions. To determine the value clusters, factor analysis was carried out on the survey data. The factors were extracted by using the Principal Component Analysis with the Varimax Rotation technique.

Reliability analysis (Crombach's Alpha) was used to determine the homogeneity (internal consistency) of the questions in each factor. The analysis was done for each of the factors as identified by the factor analysis. All value clusters, except one factor, yielded acceptable alpha coefficients. The survey yielded five clear factors:

- Value cluster 1: Professionalism – alpha of 0.841.
- Value cluster 2: Supervisor orientation to human dignity – alpha of 0.838.
- Value cluster 3: Commitment to excellence – alpha of 0.746.
- Value cluster 4: Loyalty to the department – alpha of 0.611.
- Value cluster 5: Execution of discipline – alpha of 0.431.

These factors correlate with the model identified in so far as professionalism (orientation toward values typical of professionalism), organisational customs (values typical of loyalty), lifelong learning/training (values typical of commitment to excellence) and human/ethical orientation (values typical of human rights) are concerned. The alpha of Factor 5 provided low reliability and it was decided not to interpret it further. High levels of construct validity were thus obtained.

8.6.6 Variable identification with factors and value clusters

The variables were identified with the factors or value clusters as follows:

- **Professionalism:** The greatest percentage of the respondents (81.8 per cent) responded positively to the factor concerning professionalism.
- **Human dignity:** Less than half of the respondents (48.1 per cent) responded positively to the factor concerning human dignity of supervisor.
- **Commitment to excellence:** Three quarters of the respondents (76.9 per cent) responded positively to the factor concerning commitment to excellence.
- **Loyalty to the department:** Less than 40 percent of the respondents (39.5 per cent) responded positively to the factor concerning loyalty to the department.
- **Application of discipline:** The greatest percentage of the respondents (70.6 per cent) responded positively to the factor concerning the application of discipline.

8.6.7 Variable identification with individual values

A more in-depth look, away from the collectives of the factors, into the association of the sample with individual values, revealed the following as indicated in Table 8.1:

TABLE 8.1: RESPONDENTS' IDENTIFICATION WITH VALUES

HIGH (> 60%)	AVERAGE (40–60%)	POOR (< 40%)
Accountability (74.9%) Organisational competence (88.3%) Ethics (87.7%) Discipline (82.5%) Versatility (87.0%) Acceptance of authority (77.9%) Courage (83.1%) Courtesy (80.4%) Obedience to seniors (87.4%) Self-discipline (69.1%) Developmental-oriented (67.2%) Life-long learning (75.7%) Military bearing (61.2%) Chain of command (68.0%) Teamwork (64.7%) Respect for freedom/ human life (82.6%) Patriotism (77.5%)	Commitment to task (59.5%) Commitment to colleagues (53.2%) Respect for cultural differences (53.9%) Integrity (57.6%) No rank misuse (47.6%) Impartial (76.5%) No discrimination against the disabled (47.8%) No poor excuses (44.5%) Manage according to policy (58.3%) Fair practices (55.1%)	Loyalty (33.1%) Pride (31.3%) Non-racial discrimination (39.9%) Spreading of rumours (19.6%) Non-gender discrimination (87.4%)

Values expected of an efficient organisation, such as organisational competence, ethics, discipline, acceptance of authority, courage, teamwork, obedience, self-discipline and patriotism, showed high association from members. Other values expected of an efficient organisation, such as loyalty and pride in the department, however, showed a very low association by its members. Discrimination also showed a very low association. This should clearly indicate towards potential problems within the department.

8.6.8 Conclusions of the investigation

Seventy per cent or more of the entire sample indicated a positive association with the factors of professionalism, commitment to excellence and the maintenance of discipline. This should be regarded as positive for the department and serves as an indication that measures applied to achieve this have been successful.

Half or less of the entire sample indicated a negative perception towards the factor 'supervisors/leaders' fulfilment of human dignity and loyalty to the department. The negative perception regarding loyalty indicates serious problems. An organisation cannot be efficient if it cannot depend on the loyalty of its members.

8.6.9 Maintaining a culture

Once a culture is in place the tendency is to maintain it. Management and employees perpetuate the rituals and myths that constantly reaffirm the organisational culture. Rituals are systematic and programmed routines, such as job procedures, of everyday life in the organisation and bring meaning to what may otherwise be perceived as chaos. Myths contain a narrative of events about the origin and development of the organisation. It is important that when an organisation's culture needs to be changed, as in the process of transformation, new myths and rituals need to be introduced and perpetuated.

8.6.10 Creating a new organisational culture

When it becomes necessary to change the organisational culture of a poor-performing public organisation to one that is performing optimally, it does not help to drastically change the whole of the culture. Too many skills and too much experience have been gained over time to simply ignore them. Also, much of the knowledge necessary for change and development can be found within an organisation. Therefore, it is necessary to make use of such knowledge, experience and skills.

In recent years, many public organisations have adopted a specific model to accomplish the change and development necessary to transform into dynamic organisations that not only deliver public products, goods and services optimally, but also provide a stimulating working environment for a transformed, diverse work force.

The model, called the *Learning Organisation*, was first outlined by Senge (1990; 1994) in his book, *The Fifth Discipline*. The five disciplines of the

Learning Organisation are as follows:
- personal mastery;
- mental models;
- team learning;
- building shared vision;
- systems thinking.

The term 'discipline' has implications for understanding the content of each of the five disciplines, and implies a specific field of study that is not isolated from related disciplines (Van Wyk, in Fox *et al*, 2004:11). Senge (1990:10) defines discipline as a developmental path for acquiring specific skills or competencies. Therefore, each of the five disciplines represents an area of learning, while each is intimately linked to each of the other disciplines. These five disciplines jointly form a complete system of learning within an organisational environment.

Application of the five disciplines is not an event but an ongoing process. To practise any one of the disciplines successfully requires that one becomes a lifelong learner. In the context of this book, learning may be defined as any relatively permanent change in behaviour that occurs as a result of experience.

The learning process helps one to adapt to and master one's environment. By changing one's behaviour in order to accommodate changing conditions, one becomes a responsible citizen and productive employee (Robbins, 1984:21–23). However, learning is built upon the law of effect, which states that behaviour is a function of its consequences. Behaviour followed by a favourable consequence tends to be repeated, while behaviour followed by an unfavourable consequence tends not to be repeated. In this context, 'consequence' refers to anything a person considers rewarding.

When learning takes place in graduated steps, it is said to be **shaped**. Managers shape employee behaviour by systematically reinforcing, by way of rewards, each successive step that moves the employee closer to the desired behaviour. Shaping does much of employee learning. When we refer to learning through mistakes or learning by trial and error, we are referring to shaping.

In addition to shaping, much of what employees learn is the result of observing others and **modelling** their behaviour after them. While shaping is usually a slow learning process, modelling can produce rapid and complex behavioural changes. For example, new employees who want to be successful in their job are likely to look for someone who is successful and in high regard and then attempt to imitate that person's behaviour. As their performances improve (a favourable consequence), their behaviour is likely to change to reflect what they have seen work for the other person.

In general, an individual enters an organisation with a relatively established set of **values** and **attitudes** and a substantially entrenched **personality**. An employee's values, attitudes and personality are basically givens at the time she or he enters the organisation. The way that employees interpret their work environment (**perception**) will influence their level of **motivation**, what they learn on the job and, eventually, their individual work (organisational) behaviour. Also, an individual's behaviour is influenced by his or her **ability**, that is, the talents and skills that person has when she or he joins the organisation. This will alter over time.

Personal mastery

Personal mastery is the process of continually clarifying and deepening personal vision, focusing energies, developing patience and experiencing reality objectively (Senge, 1990:7). The learning organisation creates space within which a person can spend time with herself or himself.

Mental models

Mental models or mind maps are ingrained assumptions, generalisations or mental pictures or images that influence the way people understand the world and how they act or react (Senge, 1990:8). They are sometimes identified as stereotypes or paradigms. In the workplace, mental models are created through an indirect process of observing others and their behaviour towards certain issues, people, processes or structures in the working environment. When an individual has encountered or identified mental models (or assumptions), she or he may adopt and reinforce them; dismiss them as yet another assumption; or deal with them within the organisational environment and constructively destroy them.

Team learning

Teams, and not individuals, are the fundamental learning units of the modern organisation. Team learning is similar to teamwork, team development and team building, but not synonymous with any of them. Team learning is the process that involves in groups of people attempting to complete a task together and where learning occurs through past errors and collective experience. Team learning cannot take place if teams are unable to learn with and from each other.

Building shared vision

Shared vision involves the skills of unearthing shared 'pictures of the future' that foster commitment and involvement rather than compliance (Senge, 1990:9). Building shared vision does not involve the typical process of merely transmitting the organisation's vision to employees. Rather, management should find out what core values are shared by people within the organisation and by those in their environment. This means co-creating, rather than selling or telling a vision for the organisation, at the same time ensuring that it is in accordance with the overall vision of government.

Systems thinking

This concerns the ability to place all the various parts of the organisation and its events into a system. In this way, an understanding of the linkages and cause-and-effect networks may be identified and worked on proactively. Everything can be placed within larger or smaller systems. A smaller system, such as a section, could form part of a larger system, such as a directorate, which could form part of yet a larger system, such as a department, which could be part of still a larger system, such as a civil service. One could go on in this way. The point is that all of these and other systems are bound by invisible fabrics of interrelated actions that often take many years to play out their efforts on each other to their full extent. Also, each person is part of this system of links and events and finds it difficult to observe the whole pattern of change. Human beings tend to focus on smaller, more specific events as isolated parts of the system.

Systems thinking is a device that has been developed over time to enable managers to observe the whole pattern more clearly and to assist them in seeing how to change it effectively.

8.7 Codes of conduct

All spheres of government in South Africa have been given codes of conduct. The basis of the public service code of conduct is contained in Chapter 10 of the Constitution and is applicable to the administrations within every sphere of government, organs of state and public enterprises.

8.7.1 Basic values and principles concerning public servants

The public service is directed by the democratic values and principles entrenched in the Constitution. Those principles were listed in section 8.5 of this chapter. Appointment to the public service of a number of persons on policy grounds is possible, but national legislation regulates these appointments.

National legislation ensures the promotion of these values and principles. As an example, the code of conduct for municipal staff members forms a part of the Municipal Systems Act (Act 32 of 2000) as a schedule.

8.7.2 Code of conduct for municipal staff members

The code, based on the values and principles contained in the Constitution, prescribes in detail what is expected of a municipal employee. The following are the most important provisions:

- Municipal members of staff must at all times loyally execute the lawful policies of the municipal council, and perform the functions of office in good faith, diligently, honestly and in a transparent manner. Further, they must act in the best interests of the municipality in such a way that the credibility and integrity of the municipality are not compromised, and must also act impartially and treat all people, including other members of staff, equally and without favour or prejudice.
- Municipal members of staff are employed in a developmental local system. They, therefore, must cultivate a culture of commitment to serving the public and a collective sense of responsibility for performance, pursuant to standards and targets, and promote and strive to implement the basic values and principles of public administration as provided in the Constitution.
- They have to obtain copies of and information concerning the municipality's integrated development plan within the ambit of their job descriptions, seek to implement the objectives in the development plan, and achieve the performance targets set out for each performance indicator. They also have to participate in the overall performance management system for the municipality, as well as their own individual performance appraisal and reward system, so as to maximise the ability of the municipality as a whole to achieve its objectives and to improve the quality of life of its residents.
- As far as personal gain is concerned, members of staff of a municipality may not use their positions or privileges or information obtained as

members of staff for private gain or to improperly benefit someone else. They may also not take a decision on behalf of the municipality regarding a matter in which they or their spouses, partners or business associates have a direct or indirect personal or private business interest.

- Further, they may not obtain a financial interest in any business of the municipality or be engaged in any business, trade or profession other than the work of the municipality.
- Members of staff who, or whose spouses, partners, business associates or close family members have acquired or stand to acquire any direct benefit from a contract concluded with the municipality must disclose in writing full particulars of the benefit to the council. This does not apply to a benefit that members of staff or spouses, partners, business associates or close family members have or acquire in common with all other residents of the municipality
- Municipal members of staff may not without permission disclose to any unauthorised person any privileged or confidential information acquired as members of staff. Privileged or confidential information in this context means information
  - determined by the municipal council or any structure of functionary of the municipality as privileged or confidential;
  - discussed in closed council or of committee of the council;
  - when disclosed would violate a person's right of privacy; or
  - declared to be privileged, confidential or secret in terms of any law.

  This does not derogate from anybody's right of access to information in terms of national legislation.
- Municipal members of staff may not unduly influence or attempt to influence the council or a structure or functionary of the council with a view to obtaining any appointment, promotion, privilege, advantage or benefit for themselves, a family member, friend or associate. They may also not mislead or attempt to mislead the council or a structure or functionary of the council in its consideration of any matter. They may further not be involved in a business venture with a councillor without the prior written consent of the council.
- Municipal members of staff may not request, solicit or accept any reward, gift or favour for persuading the council or any structure or functionary of the council regarding the exercise of any power or the performance of any duty; for making a representation to the council,

structure or functionary of the council; disclosing any privileged or confidential information; or for doing or not doing anything within the powers and duties of those members of staff.

- It must immediately be reported to a superior official or to the speaker of the council regarding any offer which, if accepted by a member of staff, would constitute a breach in this regard.
- Municipal members of staff may not use, take, acquire or benefit from any property or asset owned, controlled or managed by the municipality to which they have no right.
- Municipal members of staff may not be in arrears to the municipality for rates and service charges for a period longer that three months, and a municipality may deduct any outstanding amounts from their salaries after that period.
- Municipal members of staff may not participate in elections of the council other than in an official capacity or pursuant to a constitutional right.
- No municipal member of staff may embark on any action amounting to sexual harassment.
- Whenever municipal members of staff have reasonable grounds for believing that there has been a breach of the code, they must immediately report the matter to a superior officer or to the speaker of the council.
- Municipal members of staff are expected to comply in every respect with their conditions of employment and to refrain from any conduct that would give just cause for discipline.

8.8 Standards of conduct

The organised local governments and trade unions have agreed on a uniform disciplinary procedure that applies to all employers and employees within the scope of the South African Local Government Bargaining Council. Maintaining discipline is the responsibility of management and falls within the control function of all supervisory officers. The principles of natural justice and fair procedure are observed.

Employees must comply in all respects with their conditions of service and collective agreements, as well as related regulations relating to order, policy and practice, and refrain from conduct that would give cause for disciplinary action. In particular, employees must:

- attend work regularly and punctually;
- comply with the reasonable dress and uniform requirements of the employer;
- perform their tasks and responsibilities diligently, carefully and to the best of their ability;
- obey lawful and reasonable instructions given by anyone authorised to do so;
- conduct themselves with honesty and integrity;
- in advance request permission for leave of absence from duty;
- refrain from being absent from duty without leave or prior permission, except on legitimate cause;
- refrain from accepting other employment outside of normal working hours without prior permission of the head of department or municipal manager, who may not withhold permission unreasonably;
- refrain from rude, abusive, insolent, provocative, intimidatory or aggressive behaviour towards a superior, fellow employee or member of the public;
- refrain from wilful or negligent behaviour that may result in the damage of property;
- refrain from participating individually or collectively in any form of action that will have the effect of disrupting the operations of the employer, except for action in terms of the Labour Relations Act;
- refrain from wrongfully disclosing privileged information;
- refrain from consuming alcohol or using intoxicating drugs while on duty.

At a disciplinary inquiry regarding breach of the Standard of Conduct, regulating the general conduct of local council employees and promulgated in the Local Government Laws Amendment Act 19 of 2008, the presiding officer has the power to impose any of the following sanctions:

- a written warning;
- a final written warning;
- transfer to another position, either with or without financial loss;
- suspension without pay for a maximum of fourteen days spread over a period of three monthly pay periods;
- withholding any salary increment for a maximum period of twelve months;
- demotion to another post with or without financial loss;
- dismissal.

The Standard Code of Conduct, on the one hand, spells out in greater detail what is contained in the Constitution, and on the other hand provides new aspects of what is expected from employees in the course of their employment in public service.

8.9 Code of ethics

The code of ethics adopted by Telkom, the telecommunications parastatal, is quite uncomplicated and to the point (abridged: www.telkom.co.za/about_us/human_resources/code_of_ethics.html):

- It is critical for each organisation to guide the conduct of its employees in their relationships with various stakeholders in line with its value system. Telkom embraces the following values:
  We are proud and passionate about who we are and what we do.
  We will act with honesty and integrity.
  We will promote an entrepreneurial and innovative spirit.
  We will treasure diversity.
  We will not sacrifice or give up on any of our values.
- To support the values and to ensure good corporate governance, we implemented a Business Code of Ethics. It also informs employees of acceptable behaviour and conduct. The Business Code of Ethics also seeks to guide our conduct and behaviour in terms of fairness, justice and ethical standards and to ensure that the integrity of Telkom is not compromised in any way.
- It is expected of each employee to apply sound judgment in deciding on the most ethical means of dealing with any given situation involving customers, competitors, suppliers, the public, fellow employees and company matters in general. Whenever employees are uncertain on how to deal with a situation, they are encouraged to seek guidance from their seniors.

Although this code is more in line in what is usually formulated in the corporate world, because Telkom is a government enterprise its core values coincide with the typical code of conduct found in public institutions.

8.10 Affirmative action

It is argued that public institutions in complex societies like South Africa should be demographically representative of the population if they are to be effective and responsive. In contrast, it is argued that such measures are not effective and lead to negative discrimination. As provided for in the Constitution, public institutions must be representative of South African society. In addition to the prime reason that the inequalities caused by past discrimination have to be corrected, there are several reasons to ensure representative public institutions through affirmative action (Schwella *et al*, 1996:90–91):

- The first is based on the principle of equal opportunity. All citizens, despite their group affiliation, should have an equal opportunity to be employed in the public sector.
- Secondly, careers in the public service are regarded as a public good and communal property to which everybody can claim a right. It is argued that all citizens must be given the opportunity to serve the fellow members of their communities if they choose to do so. Such opportunities will afford citizens access to a political education enhancing their quality of citizenship.
- A third reason is the notion that increased representation will enhance the legitimacy of the management of public institutions.
- Fourthly, it is argued that if the composition of a public institution's human resources reflects that of society, it may be assumed that officials will be more responsive to people's needs.
- Finally, the argument supporting change favours affirmative action. It is reasoned that more representative official structures create opportunities to change social and economic structures. The preferential treatment of specified groups should contribute towards reducing prejudices, thereby effecting the change the authorities need to improve the social and economic fortunes of previously disadvantaged groups.

However, although there is general agreement with the benefits that increased representation will bring, and with the reasons for affirmative action, a cautious approach is recommended. It may be asked whether representatives from previously disadvantaged groups are expected to address problems differently, and whether they are able to legitimately change policies and decisions to favour people from their groups impartially and with integrity.

Expertise and competency are the overriding needs of public institutions. Policies and programmes relegating these qualities to a secondary position could be potentially damaging to effective public goods and service delivery. It is difficult to argue that representation will increase effectiveness in public goods and service delivery in all public sector functions, especially those of a highly technical nature.

Using statistics to set goals for representation, deciding which disadvantaged groups qualify for preferential treatment, and deciding when criteria for representation have been met, are open to various and different interpretations.

In attempting to build non-racial societies, continued emphasis on specific group identities may create division. Affirmative action could encumber, rather than foster, the forging of a common national identity.

Finally, it is sometimes argued that attempts to reach representation through intervention may harm the intended beneficiaries. Incorrect assumptions about quality and merit of beneficiaries and the creation of perceptions of dependency and entitlement are real issues.

Although it is generally accepted that affirmative action should not be a permanent feature of public human resource policy, i.e. it should run for a given period of time and should then be allowed to lapse over time, the timing of such action depends on the circumstances in the country concerned. However, the fact remains that affirmative action should eventually be terminated, rather sooner than later.

The implementation of affirmative action is a given in South African society, and some of its benefits as well as some of its challenges are becoming more and more apparent. An additional difficulty is that it is not always clear whether affirmative employment action arises out of the requirement to correct past discriminatory practices or whether it is a result of nepotism.

8.11 Nepotism

There are a number of definitions of nepotism:

- favouritism shown to relatives or close friends by those in power (as by giving them jobs);
- the showing of favouritism for relatives or friends based upon that relationship, rather than on an objective evaluation of ability or suitability;
- participating in decisions that would involve a direct benefit or

detriment to a relative as defined by law and policy;
- in generational nepotism, deceased parents may cause their children to get promoted;
- unfair practices in which people in power give positions in a government or organisation to their relatives or friends, rather than to any other persons;
- patronage bestowed, or favouritism shown, on the basis of family relationships, as in business or politics;
- the practice of keeping offices and privileges within a family.

In the model of participatory democracy agreed on by South African society, nepotism counteracts the fundamental principles and values enshrined in the Constitution.

8.12 Racism

The scientific and religious perceptions of race have a long history. As far as South Africa is concerned, it is usual to start an investigation into racism from around the middle of the 16th century and later eras of colonisation when the first Europeans settled permanently at the southern tip of Africa.

In 1652, the Dutch East India Company created a refreshment station for ships on their way to and from the East. This eventually became a Dutch colony, which remained relatively poverty-stricken. After 50 years, there were only about two thousand white settlers, and from the outset they were always a minority group. The colony grew steadily, with settlers – who were mostly farmers but also regarded themselves as lay missionaries – moving further and further away from Cape Town. They were mainly Dutch Calvinists, with a sprinkling of German Protestants and French Huguenots. They brought to Africa a tradition of dissent and called themselves Afrikaners (people from Africa). As pilgrims moving to a promised land, they also believed that they were placed here to convert to Christianity the African population they encountered.

In 1806, during the Napoleonic Wars, the British government permanently annexed the colony. This was the start of a long history of friction between the British and Afrikaners. After slavery was abolished in 1834, some five thousand settlers (and about the same number of non-white servants) moved inland and settled land that later became the Orange Free State, Natal and Transvaal. Although the designation 'Afrikaner' was still used, the inhabitants of these new territories called themselves 'burgers' and the 'Boer Nation'.

Racism was a way of life for both the colonisers and Boers. The majority of the religious denominations to which the generally devout Boers adhered also tolerated racism on scriptural grounds. In 1834, Britain established a second colony (together with the Cape Colony) when it annexed Natal, but in 1852 and 1854 it agreed to the independence of the Orange Free State and Transvaal republics. However, in an attempt to create a federation of South African states, Britain annexed the Transvaal, which led to the First War of Independence of 1881. After their defeat at Majuba, the British authorities agreed to the independence of the Transvaal.

The final confrontation between Britain and the Boers was the Anglo-Boer War of 1899–1902. Some years after the defeat of the two republics, negotiations got under way for the unification of the four territories and were later finalised by the granting of independent self-rule to the Union of South Africa in 1910. The Constitution of the Union perpetuated racism, as black (non-white) South Africans were excluded from political rights. Various political parties and coalitions ruled the Union, and in 1948 the National Party gained power and set about institutionalising racism.

Racism is the belief of some people that things such as human abilities depend on race and that some races are superior to others. It also refers to things like aggressive behaviour and speech showing hostility between races. A **racist** is a believer in racism, especially one who is hostile, disparaging or discriminatory towards races thought to be inferior. Racism manifests itself in various ways, some of which are summarised below (Kriel, 2009:2):

- **Physical violence:** This is the worst manifestation of racism. There have also been many instances of violent, explicit and implicit racism in all parts of the country.
- **Emotional violence:** This occurs when people's human dignity is not recognised by treating them inhumanely because of the colour of their skin.
- **Economic violence:** This occurs when, for example, people are deprived of opportunities and advancement because of the colour of their skin.
- **Prejudice:** This is a result of many states of mind, such as narrow-mindedness, intolerance, bias and prejudgment of one person towards another based on the colour of that person's skin.

Racism is a universal phenomenon that negatively affects human relations in all spheres of life. In South Africa, entrenched racism was a fact of life for over 300 years. However, as observed by Cilliers (2008:11), it is difficult to understand the perversities taking place in South African society, which is also renowned for its spirit of *Ubuntu*. Perhaps the devastating impact of apartheid on society has been underestimated or perhaps it was not buried deep enough.

Racism is acquired behaviour, resulting from the environment in which a person is born and lives. Nobody is born a racist. Therefore, it is obvious that the circumstances in the country that cause people to feel they are being discriminated against due to their race will have to be addressed.

In 2008, two black organisations made formal complaints to the Human Rights Commission of racism on the part of two newspapers. In terms of the South African Constitution, racism is an abuse of human rights (see Legum, 2009:1). The commission decided that since the two papers mentioned (both of a broad liberal tradition) was only a part of a much wider industry, it would be unfair and unproductive to limit the inquiry to them and the examples quoted against them.

The research sanctioned by the commission pinpointed examples of practices that could reinforce racism. The result was that most media moved out of the discussion and would not attend public hearings. After they were subpoenaed, many came to the conclusion that their right of freedom of speech was being undermined and that the South African government was on its way to totalitarian rule.

Legum (2009:1) is of the opinion that racism, in its widest and most useful meaning, cannot be proved, only recognised. Overt race prejudice and discrimination, such as name-calling, race attacks and exclusion on the grounds of race, can be proved but are only one aspect of racism. They can be defined and dealt with under equality laws. So, one of the outcomes of the media hearings was to widen mutual understanding to create a fuller picture, to create a common language in order to recognise and develop good practice around race in the media. For example, although the commission could have started with its own definition of racism, it was decided to develop one through the process.

South Africa's transition from its traumatic history could easily be underestimated, and cannot be without pain for white people. The expectation that they would be allowed to adapt at a pace that suited them, as in the Mandela era, was not realistic. It may not be sufficient to expect Western models of relying on 'the markets', or on painfully slow self-regulation processes, to change profoundly dangerous practices.

PRINCIPLES, VALUES AND NORMS PRESENTED IN THIS CHAPTER

Finance in participatory democracy
Financial interests of all citizens
Collective financial needs
Reasonable
Social equity
Efficient and effective
Optimally
Participation in public financial maters
Responsive
Sensitive
Transparency
Graft, bribery and corruption
Mismanagement and maladministration
Need-driven and greed-driven
Illegal acts
Accountability
Democratic values and principles of public human resource management
Professionalism
Human dignity
Commitment to excellence
Loyalty
Discipline
Personal mastery
Mental models
Team learning
Building shared vision
Systems thinking
Principles of service of public servants
Values and principles in codes and standards of conduct
Parastatal code of ethics
Equal opportunity
Nepotism
Racism

Having studied this chapter, how would you now answer the question posed at the beginning?

Select any five of the terms that you regard as the most important ones, and relate in what way each of them has a negative effect on public goods and service delivery.

Chapter 9

Future perspectives

IN THIS CHAPTER

After reading this chapter, you should be able to:

- discuss the meaning of societal values;
- provide a definition of social responsibility;
- define constitutionalism;
- discuss the value of democratic representation;
- discuss the importance of economic values and general values;
- outline South Africa's progress towards participatory democracy.

Before studying this chapter, see if you can answer the following question:
How important are the terms discussed in this chapter?

Depending on the interpretation one gets liars, damn liars and statisticians

9.1 Introduction

As discussed, ethics generally refers to rules or principles that define right and wrong conduct. Ethical action and behaviour form the foundation of all actions in the fields of political and corporate management, whether it concerns the natural environment, information, human resources or finance. It would seem logical that governments, their administrations and their citizens have learnt lessons from the dire consequences of unethical behaviour. This should be especially true for developing nations. However, the daily news is full of cases of individuals, agencies and countries involved in unethical and immoral acts and behaviour. Optimum public management is not sustainable if high moral values are not maintained. This should be a product of a shared system of values, universally accepted codes of conduct and respect for human rights and the natural environment (adapted from Fox, 2006:17–22).

This chapter focuses on societal values, which are either unchanging or change very little over time. Here the concern is with the ethical behaviour, in general, of various actors in public institutions. A system of values formulated and applied in the course of strategic planning and management is specific to an individual institution. The discussions here are of a basic nature.

9.2 Social responsibility

Although social responsibility does not play a pivotal part in all organisations, it does so in many and should form part of the value system of every public institution. The term 'social responsibility' has been defined in many ways. It has been called 'profit-making only', 'beyond profit-making', 'voluntary action', 'concern for the broader social system' and 'social responsiveness'. Usually, attention is paid to the extreme definitions: at the one extreme there is the purely economic view that the only social responsibility of any management, depending on its environment, is to reach objectives optimally or to maximise public goods and service delivery. At the other extreme is the socio-economic stance that a management's responsibility goes beyond purely reaching objectives or merely performing, to include preserving and improving the welfare of society.

9.2.1 The economic approach

Supporters of this view maintain that institutions' primary responsibility is to operate their activities in the best interests of their political superiors and the interests of appointed senior officials. In most cases, political office bearers have a single interest, that is, adherence to the party political stance. It is contended that any time institutions decide to spend their resources for the 'social good' beyond statutory requirements they are unnecessarily adding to budgetary costs. Those costs are then passed on to rate- and taxpayers through higher rates and taxes or scaled-down delivery of goods and services.

9.2.2 The socio-economic approach

According to this view, an institution's social responsibility goes beyond mere goods and service delivery or reaching objectives to preserving and improving the welfare of society. This view is based on the assumption that society's expectations of private, community-based and public organisations have changed. These organisations are not independent entities responsible only to stockholders, governments and donors. They have a responsibility to the broader society that endorses their creation and maintenance through laws, regulations and policies and supports them through buying or making use of their products and services. An increasing number of organisations around the world are taking their social responsibilities seriously. In a survey of business owners, for example, it was found that 68 per cent would continue socially responsible practices even if they found that those activities were cutting into profits.

In developing societies and emerging economies it may be difficult to have a universal socio-economic approach because of the day-to-day struggle of many organisations merely to survive. This does not mean that social responsibility should not be part of their system of core values.

9.2.3 From obligations to responsiveness

Social responsibility is an institution's obligation, beyond that required by law, policies or economics, to pursue long-term objectives that are good for society. This assumes that all organisations will obey all the relevant laws, regulations and policies. Also, they are viewed as moral agents: in their efforts to do good for society, they differentiate between right and wrong and, therefore, have a social responsibility. Finally, social responsibility presupposes that organisations are responsive to the needs of, and the changes in, society.

9.2.4 Social obligation

Social obligation refers to the fact that an institution is obliged to meet its legal, social, political and economic responsibilities. In an approach of social obligation, an institution pursues social goals to the extent that they merely contribute to its objectives, whether they are social or economic. This is based on the economic approach of social responsibility. In contrast to social obligation, both social responsibility and social responsiveness go beyond meeting basic legal, economic and other standards.

Social responsibility adds an ethical imperative to do those things that make society better and not to do those that could make it worse. A socially responsive institution goes beyond what it must do by law or chooses to do only because it makes economic sense to do what it can to help improve society because that is the right, or ethical, thing to do. Social responsibility requires an institution to determine what is right or wrong, and to make ethical decisions and engage in ethical activities. A socially responsible institution does what is right because it believes it has a responsibility to act in that way.

9.2.5 Social responsiveness

Social responsiveness refers to an institution's capacity to be sensitive to the needs of, and to adapt to, changing societal conditions. Social responsiveness emphasises the fact that managements and other leaders make decisions about the societal actions in which they engage. A socially responsive institution performs in this manner because of its desire to satisfy certain social needs. Social responsiveness is based on social values.

In general, social responsibility and social responsiveness may be contrasted as follows:

	Social Responsibility	**Social Responsiveness**
Major considerations	Ethical	Pragmatic
Focus	Ends	Means
Emphasis	Obligation	Responses
Decision framework	Long term	Medium to short term

9.3 Social responsibility and performance

A number of research studies have investigated performance in the context of social responsibility. The majority have found a positive relationship between social commitment and performance. However, one should not make compelling assumptions from these findings. Most of the studies determined a company's performance by analysing the content of annual reports, citations of social actions in news articles or public perception reputation indexes. Although measures of performance are more objective, they are usually used to indicate only short-term economic performance.

Usually, the impact of an institution's efficiency takes some years to become apparent. When there is a time lag, studies using short-term financial measures are not likely to show valid results. Also, if the results show that social involvement and performance are positively related, this would not necessarily signify that social involvement caused higher performance. At least one study found that when the 'flawed' empirical analyses in such studies were corrected, social responsibility actually had a negative impact on performance.

9.4 Constitutionalism

Constitutionalism requires that all actions by a country's organisations should be in accordance with their country's constitution. In a democratic society, the constitution provides for the rights and obligations of citizens, the state and its officials. It attempts to protect individual rights, entrench democratic governance and ensure proper guidance in organisations.

The Constitution is South Africa's supreme authority, and all parties must comply with its provisions. In cases of general provisions, supporting legislation is put into place to specify such provisions. The Constitution also provides for courts in which such laws can be analysed as to their constitutionality. Citizens are also able to enforce their rights through such courts.

In an effort to rationalise the traditional setup of 'supreme courts', the South African Parliament found it necessary to contemplate an amendment to the Constitution so as to make provision for the appointment of two deputy presidents in the Supreme Court of Appeal and for the conversion of the various high courts into a single High Court of South Africa. The various divisions of the High Court may rule on constitutional matters, except those matters on which only the Constitutional Court may rule. The Constitutional Court is the highest court in constitutional matters. The Constitutional Court (in Chapter 8) may rule on the following:

- disputes between organs of state and the national and provincial spheres in terms of the constitutional status, powers and functions of any of those organs of state;
- the constitutionality of any legislation of the national and provincial legislatures, in constitutionally provided cases;
- the constitutionality of amendments to the Constitution;
- whether the President or Parliament has failed to fulfil a constitutional obligation;
- the certification of a provincial constitution.

The Constitutional Court is the final authority to rule on questions of whether provincial legislation or action taken by the President is constitutional. Rulings of unconstitutionality given by the Supreme Court of Appeal or High Court may become effective only after being upheld by the Constitutional Court.

The Constitution is the cornerstone of democracy in South Africa. It entrenches the rights of all citizens and upholds the democratic values of freedom, equality and human dignity. The Constitutional Court, then, defends the constitutional rights of citizens and protects them from unconstitutional actions by individuals and organisations in all sections of society.

9.5 Values of democratic representation

Democratic values underpin the ideals of popularly elected, representative systems of governance. The following are usually considered as democratic values:

- **Representation**, as a value, requires that all organisations, whether private or public, represent their customers and beneficiaries. Organisations should have empathy with those they serve, and view matters from their perspective. It is also necessary that organisations reflect the composition of the population in occupational groups and at hierarchical levels.
- **Legitimacy** requires that actions of employees enhance the acceptance of decisions and programmes by the people who are served. Organisations should consider society's needs, and their actions should be in line with the expectations of legal and moral conduct. The legitimacy of government action should not be confused with the **legality** of such action. A government may act quite legally in terms

of the country's legislation at that time, but need not necessary enjoy legitimacy from its citizens or from the international community.

- **Transparency** refers to the extent to which the performance of public sector organisations and the actions of public servants are open to public scrutiny. Transparency requires open, honest, and publicly visible processes and actions by public servants.

9.6 Economic values

Public sector institutions use scarce societal resources in fulfilling their economic role and delivering essential products, goods and services. The extent to which these institutions are able to use their economic clout to influence the use of scarce resources depends on national economic policy and the country's level of development. Even in developed, market-oriented countries, public sector institutions complying with standard economic values and tenets play an important part in the economy. The extent of their participation emphasises the need for public sector compliance with universally accepted economic practices:

- **Effectiveness** reflects the extent to which stated objectives have been or are being met. Therefore, selected and appointed public managers should strive towards qualitative and quantitative objectives derived from policies and incorporated into programmes. Meeting qualitative and quantitative requirements reflects high effectiveness, while lesser performance indicates diminished effectiveness.
- **Efficiency** refers to the *optimal use* of scarce public resources in reaching policy and programme objectives. Efficiency is measured by the ratio of input to output. Cost–benefit analysis, and an intolerance of waste, bureaucracy and corruption quantify and strengthen the intrinsic value of efficiency. 'Value for money' drives are often associated with measures to improve efficiency.
- **Productivity** is a value related to effectiveness and efficiency. It may be defined as the delivery of products, goods and services, offset by the resources consumed in the process.

Measuring effectiveness, efficiency and productivity is often more complicated in the public sector than in the private sector. This is so because of the complexity of goals and objectives aimed at improving quality of life. Often, conflicting assessments are made because of the public sector's highly politicised context. However, it remains important to strive towards improved performance.

9.7 Social equity

There is no final, finite or exhaustive list of values citizens have to consider when taking action (Schwella *et al*, 1996:17). This is due to the dynamic societal context within which public managers have to make decisions.

Social equity aims at fairness and justice in decision-making actions. Equitable actions require considered judgment for justice to prevail. In some cases, this may require using discretion to minimise negative or damaging consequences resulting from strict, rigid application of laws, policies or regulations. Social equity requires a balanced approach to ensure that individuals or groups are not disadvantaged. It is based on empathy and understanding for all, with special attention being paid to the powerless, disadvantaged and underprivileged.

9.8 The rule of law

The rule of law represents the principle that no person is above the law (refer to www.butterworths.co.za/about-us/rule-of-law/default.aspx). It follows logically from the idea that truth, and therefore law, is based upon fundamental principles that cannot be created through an action but can be discovered.

The principle that government is legitimately exercised only in accordance with established procedural steps that are referred to as a process is the most important application of law. The principle is intended as a safeguard against arbitrary government by, for example, a totalitarian leader or by mob rule. Therefore, the rule of law is hostile both to dictatorship and to anarchy.

The rule of law is an integral part of representative democracy and constitutionalism, and requires actions in terms of the constitution and other laws. It acts against arbitrariness and demands adherence to legality. It also opposes personal and collective prejudices and preferences affecting decisions and actions. In order to understand the position of legislatures, executive authorities and the judiciary in a representative democracy in relation to the rule of law, it is necessary to understand, first, the principle of separation of powers and, second the power/authority relationship between voters and their elected political representatives.

9.8.1 Separation of powers

As the representative of South Africa's citizens, Parliament enacts its legislative authority in terms of the provisions of the Constitution. It also has to ensure government by the people by choosing the President, by providing a national forum for public consideration of issues, by passing legislation and by scrutinising and overseeing executive action. Therefore, the Constitution places authority with Parliament not only to legislate, but also to ensure government of the people and to oversee activities of the executive authority.

The national executive is vested in the President. The President exercises the executive authority, together with the other members of the Cabinet, by implementing national legislation, except when the Constitution or other legislation provides otherwise. This involves developing and implementing national policy, co-ordinating the functions of government departments and administrations, preparing and initiating legislation and performing any other executive function provided for in the Constitution or in national legislation. Therefore, although the legislature oversees the executive, the executive has independent authority as provided in the Constitution and national legislation.

The judicial authority of South Africa is vested in the courts, which are **independent** and subject only to the Constitution and the law, which they apply impartially and without fear, favour or prejudice. No individual or organ of state may interfere with the functioning of the courts. Organs of state, through legislation and other measures, must assist and protect the courts to ensure their independence, impartiality, dignity, accessibility and impartiality. Finally, an order or decision issued by a court binds everyone to whom, and organs of state to which, it applies.

9.8.2 The power/authority relationship

There is not an obvious difference in the general usage of the terms 'power' and 'authority'. Gildenhuys (1993:84–85) emphasises that they do not have the same meaning as far as political relations are concerned. Authority creates a situation of obedience or submissiveness in which power is not really a factor, although authority frequently has to be supported by power, albeit with the consent of those concerned. This definition is specifically applicable in what is usually referred to as government authority. Authority is also the 'power' bestowed upon elected and appointed public officials to execute decisions of the legislature. In considering the difference in meanings between power and authority, it may be concluded that in a real democracy the actual political power is vested in the registered voters.

9.9 Progress towards participatory democracy

A research report commissioned in March 2008 by the Policy Unit of the Presidency (see Booysen, 2008:6–12) forms part of a project assessing fifteen years of democracy in South Africa. The terms of reference specified that the main objective was to be a review of the changes in political and state institutions and an assessment of the effectiveness of government measures to improve citizen access to institutions of governance and deepen their participation in political decision-making. The three secondary objectives were to review the progress made in transforming state and political institutions, to identify and assess the effectiveness of the measures implemented by government to improve citizens' participation and access to governance institutions, and to identify major trends in South Africa over the past fifteen years as well as the social currents that have driven and shaped those trends.

The research was anchored in secondary, interpretive research. No primary–empirical research was undertaken for the implementation of the project. The report utilises insights derived from academic and applied research articles and reports. It also explores a wide range of government documents, both in the domains of mapping processes of democracy and assessments of initiatives. The documents and sources included annual reports, policies and draft policies, details of White Paper processes, surveys to assess progress on particular projects, presentations to parliamentary committees and high-level speeches by and informal discussions with persons in the public sector. Finally, the report draws on public opinion surveys that assist in shedding light on the project themes of the effectiveness of participatory initiatives.

The project agreed that South Africa has been on the road of sustaining, elaborating, extending and supplementing the base democratic institutions that the country gained as from 1994. Therefore, South Africa has witnessed multi-pronged and multi-sphere action in the field of strengthening and/or elaborating the institutions of democracy. This was done in recognition of the significance of these institutions in sealing liberation and democracy, as well as in working to ensure that these institutions have enduring value for the enabling and facilitating processes of transformation and development.

South Africa has a specific type of participatory democracy in which institutions, processes and mechanisms in general work to enable both action and deliberation. Participation in democracy is advanced and bolstered through conventional and constitutionally entrenched institutions, as well as through local and national initiatives to bring about supplementary forms of access and engagement, the latter including multiple initiatives in the first decade of the 21st century. These initiatives include *izimbizo*, community development workers, *Thusong* service centres, and Project Consolidate, and span a range of phases in the process of policy and governance deliberation.

Public participation in South Africa has been characterised by cyclical movements. There are cyclical movements that are associated with electoral periods. A broader cyclical effect was also identified: from high levels of action in the early years of democracy, there followed a wave of lowering levels of public participation. Following and overlapping on this was the launch of government initiatives to bring about higher citizen engagement with the processes of government. Therefore, government in effect facilitated participation in policy and governance processes – policy implementation, monitoring and evaluation, providing feedback and identifying gaps in policy – as being realised in practice. Simultaneous with the latter process, and used in conjunction with electoral participation, were the support for (and often participation in) direct or protest action and directing of civil society inputs from the executive authority.

The study reached the conclusion that South African participatory democracy is typified by, inter alia, the continuous addition of layers of public participation in processes of policy and governance. The thrusts of these layers are often somewhat at odds with one another – for example, in supporting or challenging government. Yet South Africans appear to be largely at ease with such divergent and multiple repertoires of action. Therefore, different emerging forms add to preceding actions, rather than substitute for preceding forms.

The detailed findings elaborate, pose conditions for, and contextualise the main trends on six fronts of participatory democracy in South Africa (Booysen, 2008:9–11):

- **Institution-building and revision of base institutions:** Such institutions, especially those at national level, continue to enjoy legitimacy and relatively high esteem, even if over the years, these assessments have gradually moved down. Cyclical effects are also in play. Assessments peak at the time of elections. However, in terms of longitudinal data there was also a decline over time.

- **Representational measures and indirect democracy:** The participation of South African citizens in elections, especially in the concurrent national and provincial elections, remains high and creditable. Participation in local elections is low, yet credible by international standards, but not in decline. At the same time, voters are cynical about whether elections really make a difference to how governments react to their needs. Electoral action appears to be relatively insulated from the other modes of participation.
- **Co-optive, centre-driven management and consultation:** The mechanisms for policy and governance co-ordination and select public participation arose, on the one hand, as the result of the requirements of the time. Policy needs were largely known, the phases of public inputs into policy had mainly been completed, and there was a need on the part of government to rapidly advance processes of delivery and development. This resulted in a mostly top-down and centre-driven process that selectively called for participation, especially from elite stakeholders. The politics of personality also played a role in this development. On the other hand, the omnipresence of this system also created an environment in which many in civil society and elite from the (relatively) excluded group felt marginalised, resented not being in the centre and, in the end, rebelled. However, the system generally became enmeshed with government practices.
- **Extended and reinforced participation:** Government initiated a wide range of measures to extend its interactive interface with citizens, hoping to achieve both participation (engagement) and, through cooperation, enable developmental government. These initiatives complemented the mechanisms of policy and governance coordination. This set of actions to solicit participation and engagement were directed at civil society and professional elites, special interest groups and engagement with communities. Measures such as *izimbizo*, Project Consolidate, community development workers, and *Thusong* service centres are part of these initiatives and are mostly early phases of institutionalisation. Several interim assessments point to areas for

further development. The study found that in most instances the lack of evaluative information detracted from definite assessments of the effectiveness of those measures.

- **Direct process action:** This action was taken by citizens. The measures were twofold, i.e. to bring quality of representation into the local and other representational mechanisms, and to bring delivery and more definite transformation. Protest action was found to coexist with, rather than detract from, electoral participation at the local level.
- **Participation through mass media and government in communicative action:** The role of the mass media vis-à-vis the public was beyond the brief of the project. Diverse and extensive government communications have reached out to communities, providing essential participatory and engagement and links into government. This extended into a range of transversal, sector and sphere-specific actions. Also, the public widely utilises general mass media coverage of government, governance and policies. The research illustrates effective public uptake of government information.

South Africa is on the road to extending and potentially deepening participatory democracy. However, this road does not represent a unidirectional and an uninterrupted and increasing line. There are cyclical and other lows, and a generalised (and probably also cyclical) decline in electoral participation and in the trust and legitimacy of the base institutions of democracy. For example, this is evident in the weaknesses of elected institutions.

At the national level, there are largely credible institutions, but these are troubled by continuous problems of representation and growing issues of the credibility of representativeness. Elected provincial governments have become questioned because of their invisibility, or visibility for the wrong reasons (i.e. because of questionable public or private financial operations).

Local government, often projected as taking government to the people, has been largely unsuccessful in terms of creating effective representational mechanisms, as well as in fully facilitating local development. Concurrently, government has launched initiatives to further advance access to, and participation in, a range of phases in the process of policy-making and governance. These initiatives balance the centre-driven process of expertise-based public consultation.

Government has initiated a range of projects to extend citizen engagement with, and uptake of, public policies. Another concomitant trend is that of largely cyclical, but otherwise continuous, protest action that intersects with developmental and transformational delivery. Such trends are further enhanced by the continuous use of government and private media communication to establish either direct or indirect or mediated lines of communication between government and citizens. Therefore, on the whole and given this multi-pronged development of participatory actions, and despite occasional and sustained setbacks, it may be affirmed that South Africa is potentially making progress towards the deepening of democracy, in particular participatory democracy.

In many ways, progress has been made, in the sense that the pitfalls of running democratic government under frequently adverse socio-economic conditions, and with recognition of the limits of representative democracy, have been realised and are in the process of being potentially effectively addressed. However, in the period from the mid-1990s to 2008, judged by realised outcomes, South Africa has not made consistent, substantial and effective progress in the deepening of democracy and the operationalisation of participatory democracy.

In terms of the themes explored in the report, the period 2004–2010 has not made a substantial supplementary and subsequent contribution to the advances of the first decade of democracy.

PRINCIPLES, VALUES AND NORMS PRESENTED IN THIS CHAPTER

Social responsibility
Social responsiveness
Social obligation
Social responsibility and performance
Representation
Legality
Legitimacy
Transparency
Effectiveness
Efficiency
Productivity
Social equity
The rule of law
Separation of powers

Having studied this chapter, how would you now answer the question posed at the beginning?
Discuss in 500 words the values of democratic representation and how it relates to any one of the other terms in this chapter.

References

Printed sources

Aristotle, 2004. *The Nicomachean Ethics*. New edition, translated by J.A.K. Thompson. London: Penguin Books.

Boardman, J., Griffin, J. & Murray, O. (eds). 2001. *The Oxford Illustrated History of Greece and the Hellenistic World*. New York: Oxford University Press.

Booysen, S. 2008. 'Review of South Africa's Fifteen Years of Democracy: An Overview of Progress towards Participatory Democracy'. Unpublished draft report commissioned by the Policy Unit of the Presidency of South Africa, in association with German Technical Cooperation (GTZ).

Broodryk, J. 2005. Ubuntu *Management Philosophy*. Randburg: Knowres.

Caplin, W.D. & Dwyer, L. 2000. *Does Your Government Measure Up? Basic Tools for Local Officials and Citizens*. Syracuse, New York: Syracuse University Press.

Cilliers, J. 2008. 'In search of meaning between *Ubuntu* and *Into*: perspectives on preaching in post-apartheid South Africa'. Paper delivered at the Eighth International Conference of *Societas Homiletica* in Copenhagen.

Cilliers, J.H. 2007. 'Religious and cultural transformations and the challenges for churches: a South African perspective'. *Practical Theology in Africa* 22(2):1–19.

Cloete, J.J.N. 1992. *Public Administration and Management*. Pretoria: Van Schaik.

Constitutional Court. 2007. *FS Masiya v Director of Public Prosecutions*. Case No. CCT 54/06.

Covey, S.R. 1992. *The Seven Habits of Highly Effective People*. London: Simon & Schuster.

Darwin, C. 2004. *The Descent of Man: Selection in Relation to Sex*. New edition. London: Penguin Books.

Fox, W. 2006. *Managing Organisational Behaviour*. Cape Town: Juta

Fox, W., Schwella, E. & Wissink, H. 2004. *Public Management*. Stellenbosch: Sun Press.

Gildenhuys, J.S.H. 1993. *Public Financial Management*. Pretoria: Van Schaik.

Giliomee, H. & Mbenga, B. 2007. *Nuwe Geskiedenis van Suid-Afrika*. Cape Town: Tafelberg.

Hegel, G.W.F. 2008. *Outlines of the Philosophy of Right* (*Grundlinien der Philosophie des Rechts*). Revised edition, translated by T.M. Knox. Oxford: OUP/Oxford World's Classics.

Hobbes, T. 2008. *Leviathan*. New edition. London: Penguin Books.

Huddleston, M.W. 1992. *The Public Administration Workbook*. Second edition. New York: Longman.

Jeffreys, H. 2009. 'Waghonde moet wakker slaap'. *Die Burger*, 21 May.

Kant, I. 2005. *The Moral Law: Groundwork of the Metaphysics of Morals* (*Grundlegung zur Metaphysik der Sitten*). New edition, translated by H.J. Paton. London: Routledge Classics.

Kierkegaard, S. 2004. *Either/Or: A Fragment of Life*. New abridged edition, translated by A. Hannay. London: Penguin Books.

Kriel, K. 2009. 'Racism: definition & manifestations'. Paper delivered at the UNISA Colloquium on Race and Racism in South Africa.

Landman W. 2009. ''n Joost leen hom tot 'n uitjou'. *Die Burger*, 21 May.

Legum M. 2009. 'Media racism: the South African probe'. Unpublished paper.

Locke, J. 1993. *Two Treatises of Government*. New edition. London: Phoenix.

Louw, D.J. 2002. *Ubuntu and the Challenge of Multiculturalism in Post-apartheid South Africa*. Utrecht: Zuidam & Uithof.

Maphisa, S. 1994. *Man in Constant Search of* Ubuntu*: A Dramatist's Obsession*. Pietermaritzburg: University of Natal, AIDSA.

Mbigi, L. & Maree, J. 2005. Ubuntu: *The Spirit of African Transformation Management*. Randburg: Knowres.

Naudé, P. 2008. 'Ons is moreel nie alte slim'. *Rapport*, 4 May.

Osborne, D. & Gaebler, T. 1992. *Reinventing Government*. New York: Addison-Wesley.

Raga, K. 2009. 'Origin of ethics'. Unpublished manuscript.

Ramose, M.B. 1999. *African Philosophy Through* Ubuntu. Harare: Mond Books.

Ranney, A. 1975. *The Governing of Men*, 4th edition. Hinsdale, Illinois: Dryden.

Republic of South Africa. 1996. *Constitution of the Republic of South Africa, 1996*. Pretoria: *Government Gazette* No. 17678 of 18 December 1996.

Republic of South Africa. 2001. *Financial Intelligence Centre Act 38 of 2001*. Pretoria: *Government Gazette* No. 22886 of 3 December 2001.

Republic of South Africa. 2003. *Municipal Finance Management Act 56 of 2003*. Pretoria: *Government Gazette* No. 26019 of 13 February 2004.

Republic of South Africa. 2000. *Municipal Systems Act 32 of 2000*. Pretoria: *Government Gazette* No. 21766 of 20 November 2000.

Republic of South Africa. 2004. *Prevention and Combating of Corrupt Activities Act 12 of 2004*. Pretoria: *Government Gazette* No. 26311 of 28 April 2004.

Republic of South Africa. 2000. *Promotion of Access to Information Act 2 of 2000*. Pretoria: *Government Gazette* No. 20852 of 3 February 2000.

Republic of South Africa. 2000. *Promotion of Administrative Justice Act 3 of 2000*. Pretoria: *Government Gazette* No. 20853 of 3 February 2000.

Republic of South Africa. 2000. *Protective Disclosures Act 26 of 2000*. Pretoria: *Government Gazette* No. 21453 of 7 August 2000.

Republic of South Africa. 2000. *Public Finance Management Act 1 of 1999*. Pretoria: *Government Gazette* No. 19814 of 2 March 1999.

Republic of South Africa. 1997. White Paper on Transforming Public Service Delivery. Pretoria: *Government Gazette* No. 18340 of 1 October 1997.

Republic of South Africa. 1996. White Paper on Welfare. Pretoria: *Government Gazette* No 16934 of 2 February 1996.

Robbins, S.P. 1984. *Essentials of Organisational Behaviour*. London: Prentice Hall.

Shutte, A. 1993. *Philosophy for Africa*. Cape Town: UCT Press.

Schwella, E., Burger, J., Fox, W. & Müller, J.J. 1996. *Public Resource Management*. Cape Town: Juta.

Senge, S.M. 1990. *The Fifth Discipline: The Art & Practice of the Learning Organization*. London: Random House.

Spinoza, B. 2004. *Ethics* (*Ethica*). New edition, translated by E. Curley. London: Penguin Books.

Van Binsbergen, W. 2003. *Intercultural Encounters. African and Anthropological Lessons Toward a Philosophy of Interculturality*. Münster: Lit Verlag.

Electronic sources

About.com, 2009. 'Psychology', at psychology.about.com/od/historySof psychology/a/hist_humanistic.htm; accessed 29 July 2009.

Answers.com, 2009. 'Third World', at www.answers.com/topic/third-world; accessed 29 January 2010.

Asimow, M. 1996. 'Administrative Law under South Africa's Final Constitution: The need for an administrative justice act', *South African Law Journal* 613 (1996), at papers.ssrn.com/sol3/papers.cfm?abstract_id=10406; accessed 29 January 2010.

Chuma, W. 2008. 'Global recession bites South African economy', at www.twnafrica.org/index.php?option=com_content&view=article&id=84:globa; accessed 30 January 2010.

Clancy, R. 'Ethics of democracy', at www.cooperativeindividualism.org/clancy-robert_ethics-of-democracy.html; accessed 1 September 2009.

Columbia University Law School, 2008. *Declaration of the Rights of Man and of the Citizen* (1789), at www.hrcr.org/docs/frenchdec.html; accessed 17 March 2010.

Constitution Society, 2010. *On the Law of War and Peace* (*De Jure Belli ac Pacis*) by Hugo Grotius, at www.constitution.org/gro/djbp.htm; accessed 17 March 2010.

Hebbar, N.H. 2002. 'Ethics of Hinduism', at www.boloji.com/hinduism/032.htm; accessed 16 June 2009.

LexisNexis South Africa, 2010. 'Rule of law', at www.butterworths.co.za/about-us/rule-of-law/default.aspx; accessed 26 August 2009.

Mbeki, T. 2009. 'Statement on fraud and corruption', at www.saiga.co.za; accessed 25 May 2009.

Office of the United Nations High Commissioner for Human Rights, 2009. *International Covenant on Economic, Social and Cultural Rights* (1976), at www2.ohchr.org/english/law/cescr.htm; accessed 17 March 2009.

Office of the United Nations High Commissioner for Human Rights, 2009. *International Covenant on Civil and Political Rights* (1976), at www2.ohchr.org/english/law/ccpr.htm; accessed 17 March 2010.

Pargeter, D. 2002. 'Presentation at a forum on refugees and asylum seekers at Montmorency Uniting Church', at jmm.aaa.net.au/articles/352.htm; accessed 27 January 2010.

Parliamentary Monitoring Group, 2009. 'Public sector compliance with Public Finance Management Act', at www.pmg.org.za/node/7376; accessed 15 August 2009.

Princeton University, Department of Classics, 2004. 'Two basic Greek terms', at www.princeton.edu/~aford/terms.html; accessed 27 January 2010.

Rinkle, R. 2005. '*Stare decisis*', at www.lectlaw.com/def2/s065.htm; accessed 27 January 2010.

Schroeder, D. 2005. 'Evolutionary ethics', at www.iep.utm.edu/e/evol-eth.htm; accessed 29 July 2009.

South African Human Rights Commission (SAHRC), 2003. *Fourth Annual Economic and Social Rights Report 2000–2002*, at www.info.gov.za/view/DownloadFileAction?id=94652; accessed 17 March 2010.

Taylor, K, 1996. 'Hospitality in the Ancient Greek World', at crowdog.net/hospitality.html; accessed 27 January 2010.

Telkom SA Limited, 2009. 'Values: Code of ethics', at www.telkom.co.za/about_us/human_resources/code_of_ethics.html; accessed 27 August 2009.

United Kingdom National Archives, 2009. *Bill of Rights* (1688), at www.statutelaw.gov.uk/content.aspx?activeTextDocId=1518621; accessed 17 March 2010.

University of Cambridge, 2008. 'Investigating Atheism: Atheism & Morality', at www.investigatingatheism.info/morality.html; accessed 22 January 2010.

United States National Archives, 2009. *Bill of Rights* (1791), at www.archives.gov/exhibits/charters/bill_of_rights_transcript.html; accessed 17 March 2010.

Wikipedia, 2009. 'Administrative law', at en.wikipedia.org/wiki/Administrative_law; accessed 2 June 2009

Wikipedia, 2009. 'Common law', at en.wikipedia.org/wiki/Common_law; accessed 2 June 2009.

Wikipedia, 2009. 'Decolonization', at en.wikipedia.org/wiki/Decolonization; accessed 3 August 2009.

Wikipedia, 2009. 'Islamic ethics', at en.wikipedia.org/wiki/Islamic_ethics; accessed 27 May 2009.

Wikipedia, 2009. 'Jewish ethics', at en.wikipedia.org/wiki/Jewish_ethics; accessed 2 June 2009.

Wikipedia, 2009. '*Summum bonum*', at en.wikipedia.org/wiki/Summum_bonum; accessed 27 January 2010.

Wikipedia, 2009. 'Universal Declaration of Human Rights', at en.wikipedia.org/wiki/Universal_Declaration_of_Human_Rights; accessed 3 August 2009.

Wikipedia, 2009. 'Utilitarianism', at en.wikipedia.org/wiki/Utilitarianism; accessed 29 July 2009.

Index